Dream Notes 2003

Short and to the point Notes and Shortcuts on Microsoft's Office

by

Kirt C. Kershaw

authorHOUSE™

1663 LIBERTY DRIVE, SUITE 200
BLOOMINGTON, INDIANA 47403
(800) 839-8640
WWW.AUTHORHOUSE.COM

First published by AuthorHouse 02/03/05

ISBN: 1-4208-3014-7 (sc)

Library of Congress Control Number: 2005901065

Printed in the United States of America
Bloomington, Indiana

This book is printed on acid-free paper.

Table of Contents

About The Contents

Book's Origin

The full day of training is coming to a close as Kirt finishes writing down on the wipe board all that he has covered in class. Students have pushed their thick training manuals of the day's course off to the side, replaced with note pad and pen in hand they are busily writing down exactly what's on the board: Terms, their brief definitions and executable shortcuts.

How To Use This Book

The quickest and easiest way people communicate is with symbols. This book uses a combination of symbols and are as follows with examples of how to read them.

Legend:		Example (interpretation)
Mouse Click	/	**/Start** (click Start)
Button	(b)	**/Start (b)** (click Start button)
To	>	**/Start (b)>All Programs** (click Start button to All Programs)
Enter or Return	®	**Type in your name** ® (Type in your name & press Enter *key*)
Task Pane	TP	**TP /Blank Document *link*** (In Task Pane click the Blank Document *link*)

Dream Notes XP also available www.dreamforce.us

Word

Help – If you have any questions you can type your question up on *toolbar* in the "Type a question for help" box & hit ® Or, Help>Microsoft Office Word Help & type in your **keyword** & /Start (b) (Note: Word is defaulted to search Microsoft's online database, which is good as you get the most up to date results, but annoying if your internet speed is slow or Microsoft's server is down and hence slows you down. To turn this feature off, and have Word search your computer's database for help then: Help>Microsoft Office Word Help, <u>TP</u>: scroll down to the section "See also" & /Online Content Settings *link* & uncheck "Show contents and links…" /ok. This action will apply to ALL of your office programs and will take after you restart your office program)

Word Wrap – When you type your document & get to the end of your first line you don't have to hit ® (unless you want a new paragraph), but keep typing & Word will wrap your text for you on the next line.
   <u>Hard Returns or Paragraphs</u> – When you hit ® Word creates a paragraph for each ®. This is fine if you need extra spacing, otherwise let Word Wrap your sentences for you, otherwise other more advanced techniques will become obsolete.
   <u>Soft Returns</u> – Shift+® (forces new line break without inserting a paragraph)

Show Hide Codes – To see the background codes of your document, on *toolbar* /Show Hide (b) (and /this (b) again to turn off codes. Dots are spaces & arrows are tabs)

1st Time Customize Toolbars – The first time you use Word, Right /any (b) on any *toolbar*>Customize, /Options *tab* & check the 1st two boxes – so you can view both *toolbars* on two rows and your menus always display fully without delays. (Note: Once you set this up, the settings ought to stay permanent unless you re-install Office. Also, if you lose a *toolbar*, Right /any remaining *toolbar* & select from the list of *toolbars* "Standard" or "Formatting;" whichever of the original 2 or any others you're missing or View>Toolbars works too).

Save – When you Save your document for the 1st time Word performs a Save As! But after you Save it once, all you have to do is on *toolbar* /Save (b) & it will save without any questions.

Save As – When a document is Saved for the 1st time Word will open a small window to ask you a couple of questions before it can save your document:
   1. Where do you want to save your document: /Save in *arrow*>a place like a folder or your Desktop
   2. What is the name of your document: In File Name *box* type in the **name** of your document & /Save
   Also, if you have a document 5 pages long addressed to Sam & you want to create a copy for Cathy without having to retype it: File>Save As & rename the File **Cathy**. Now you'll have 2 documents: 1 for Sam & 1 for Cathy

Smart Tags – Little boxes that pop up in certain places for particular reasons: For example if you type in a person's name & address in Word & hover over it with your pointer, a *box* pops-up for you to / on to choose to enter this address as a Contact in Outlook 2002 Or to look up a map for this address on the internet! (Note, you have to have Microsoft's

| Mouse Click / | To > | Task Pane <u>TP</u> |

Outlook program installed on your computer to add it as a Contact)

Turn Off – For some people all those little boxes (Smart Tags), can be annoying & turn them off: Tools>AutoCorrect Options, /Smart Tags *tab* & uncheck first box "Label Text with Smart Tags," /ok. Also, Tools>Options, /View tab & uncheck Smart tags

Print Preview – If you have any question as to what will actually print /Print Preview (b), as what you see is what you get: On *toolbar* /Print Preview (b)

Print – To view print options before you print either: File>Print or Ctrl+P & select your options & /ok to print

View Full Page – Some people like to see their full page's view, including margins & Headers & Footers (if any). For this to work you'll need to be in Print Layout *view*: View>Print Layout, then on *toolbar* /Zoom *arrow*>Page Width

Selecting Text – There are several ways you can select a word or a sentence in your document for any editing purposes:
Select word by word – Ctrl+Shift+left or right arrows on *keyboard*
Line – Ctrl+/Line Or Move pointer into your left margin of your document until it point's right then /
Word – // a word
Paragraph – ///
All – Ctrl+A
Multiple Selections – Use Ctrl *key* to select multiple text scattered through your document.
Point>Home or End – You can select everything from wherever your cursors flashing>Home or End of your Document when you Ctrl+Shift+End or Ctrl+Shift+Home

AutoText – You can program Word to insert a phrase after you type its first 4 letters & hit ®: Select the text you want as AutoText & Insert>AutoText>New, /ok. Now simply type in the first 4 letters of your phrase & watch for a yellow *tag* to appear, when it does hit ® to accept it.
Delete – To delete: Insert>AutoText>AutoText & type in the first letter of your phrase & look in the window below for your complete phase & select it & /Delete (b)

Move Text – You can move your text around 2 ways:
1. Drag – Select your text & with your mouse / & drag it to wherever you want on your document.
2. Cut – Select your text & on *toolbar* /Cut (b) (your text will be cut to a clipboard that isn't visible to you unless you make it so), & / in a place with your mouse on your document & /Paste (b) (Note: when you paste any text a little Smart Tag will pop up. You can /on it & from the options listed you can change the way you just pasted your text to hold it's formatting or only paste plain text)

| Button (b) | Enter or Return ® | Close X |

Copy Text – Select your text & on *toolbar* /Copy (b) & put your cursor in another part of your document & /Paste (b) OR you can select your text & hold Ctrl *key* & drag with your mouse to another part of your document.

Clipboard – When you Cut or Copy your text it goes to the clipboard & stays there until you paste it on your document. In fact, you can have cut or copied up to 24 items on your clipboard to later paste individually, in the order you'd like, in another part of your document OR another document all together: Edit>Office Clipboard. You'll see the TP: is your clipboard & anything you cut or copy will display in it up to 24 items. After which you can then Right / any item in your clip board>Paste & or Delete.

Undo Redo – If you made a recent mistake in your document you can Undo it: On *toolbar* /Undo (b) (a blue *arrow*) AND if you Undo something & decide you want it back /Redo (b) on *toolbar*

Find & Replace – To find text or find & replace text: Edit>Find & type your text in Find *box* & check "Highlight All Items Found" & (Note: /More (b) to find case sensitive words etc.) /Find (b). To replace /Replace *tab* & in Replace *box* type what you'd like replaced & /Replace All (b) (Note: If you check "Match Case" or use the Format (b) to find & replace formatting with other types of formatting, when finished, be sure to uncheck "Match Case" & or clear the formatting for future use)

Format Text – To change the format of your text to bold, italic & color: 1ˢᵗ Select your text & Format>Font & choose your formats here & /ok when you're finished.

Quick Format – To apply the most recent 'single' format style to other text: For example, select some text & on *toolbar* /Bold (b) & now select some different text & press F4. (Again, this quick format only applies a single, most recently applied format, unless you Format>Font, in which case select as many formatting options, /ok & then select some text & hit F4. Also, for copying already formatted text to apply to other text see Format Painter…)

Format Painter – Used to copy multiple format styles from one text to another: Find some text that has some formatting (like bold, red, size 24 etc.) you'd like to copy & apply it to some plain text, then / in it so your cursor is flashing in the middle of it & on *toolbar* /Format Painter (b), then find some text & drag your brush over it. (Note: Your Format Painter will only paint once & disappear, unless you //the brush, and it won't stop painting until you / once on the brush again or hit ESC *key*)

Character Spacing – to customize spacing between characters: Select your text you want to increase or decrease spacing between characters & Format>Font, /Character Spacing *tab*, /Spacing *arrow*>Expanded (or Condensed). To raise text in a line above or below: Select your text & Format>Font, /Position *arrow*>Raised (or Lowered), /By *arrow*>a point, /ok.

Text Effects – you can apply glittering color to your text: Select your text, Format>Font, /Text Effects *tab* & select one, /ok.

Paragraph Togetherness – to keep your paragraph from splitting apart at your page break i.e. keeping all your lines of your paragraph together: / in your paragraph, Format>

Paragraph, /Line & Page Breaks *tab* & check "Keep lines together," (Note: if you turn on your codes you'll see a small square left of the paragraph – looks like a bullet, but it isn't. That indicates that, that paragraph is keeping its lines together). You can also keep 2 paragraphs from splitting up on a page break too: /in your first paragraph that you would like to keep it together with the next paragraph if there's a page break breaking them up & Format>Paragraph, /Line & Page Breaks *tab* & check "Keep with next," /ok.

Highlighter – Word has a highlighter you can use to highlight your text: On Formatting *toolbar* /the tiny down *arrow* to the right of the Highlighter (b)>select a highlighter color. Then / & drag over text you'd like highlighted. (To stop highlighting /Highlighter (b) or press ESC *key*)

Header Styles – You can apply a pre-formatted heading style to your text that is headings for paragraphs of text: Select the text that is a heading for a paragraph(s) & on Formatting *toolbar* /Style *arrow*>Heading 1, 2, 3 etc. (Note: if you decide later to use Word's "Table of Contents" or other advanced Word features, in your doc. you have to have all your headings applied using the Header Styles on from the Style *arrow*. You could cheat and apply bold & a font size like 14 to your documents headings, but then Word wouldn't recognize that and not include those headers in your "Table of Contents." Note, you can also modify the Heading 1 style: Format>Styles & Formatting TP: scroll to & Right /Heading 1>Modify & make your changes)

> Document Map – is a very helpful advanced feature for navigating your doc. if you chose to use Word's Heading styles for your headings. View>Document Map (Note: This will open up a pane that will display only your headings that have Word's Heading Styles applied to them – *see Header Styles*. Also, you can /the text in the Map *pane* & it will take you right to that heading)

> Outline View – another way of viewing & checking to see if you have Word's default Heading styles applied to your headings in your document: View>Outline, On Outline *toolbar* find & /Show Level *arrow*>Show Level 1 (Note: that is Level 1 is Word's Heading 1 style & if your document is blank then you don't have any Heading 1 style in your doc & most likely no other Headings, but do check, in which case View>Print Layout & add your apply Word's default Heading styles to your headings, again *see Header Styles*)

Styles & Formatting – You can create, apply, modify or view styles to your text in the Styles & Formatting TP on *toolbar* /Styles & Formatting (b)…

> Create – You can create your own style that includes not only a font format but also paragraph too: TP /New Style (b) & type the **name** of your new style, then select your font & its size & check "Add to template" (allows your new Style to appear in New docs.), then /Format (b)>Paragraph & set "Spacing" After>**6** pt, /ok, /ok.

> > Delete – Right /your style>Delete

> Apply – 1st select some text you'd like a preformatted style applied to, then in TP /Show *arrow*>Available styles, & / on a style like Heading 2

> Modify – If a style, like Heading 1, has too large a font, you can modify it to a smaller size: TP Right /Heading 1>Modify, /Format (b)>Font & select a size, /ok (Note: if any Heading 1 style already applied in your documents ALL of them will be updated to size 12).

> > Create Table Style – if you create a table with particular formatting or style, then create it once as a style that you can use over & over again without recreating it: Table>Table

Button (b)	Enter or Return ®	Close X

AutoFormat, /New (b) & type a **name**, then select what part of the table you'd like to work on applying a format to i.e. /Apply formatting to *arrow*>Header row, /Italics, /Bold, /Fill Color *arrow*>light color, /Apply formatting to *arrow*> Whole Table, /All Borders (b) (to apply borders to your table), check "Add to template" (allows the Style to appear in New docs.), /ok.

Apply Style – Table>Insert>Table, /AutoFormat, select your custom table style, /ok, /ok.

Tab Stops – When you hit your Tab *key* Word tabs 5-spaces (default), but you can set your Tab to stop more or less with your text aligned to the left, right or center of those stop: For example, let's say we want to create 3 columns of information like so –

Books   Author   Cost

On a blank page type **Books**. / on your Vertical Ruler to deselect your page. Just above your Vertical Ruler (if you don't have a Vertical Ruler then View>Print Layout) you'll see a little box with an L shape in it, hover over this with your mouse & it ought to say "Left Tab." If you / on it, it will toggle through other Tabs. Toggle to the "Center Tab." Then with your mouse /on the Horizontal Ruler's 3-inch mark (the Center Stop ought to be inserted, if not try again). Hit the Tab *key* & it will tab to 3-inch Tab stop, then type **Author** (Note: Author is centering off of 3-inch Center Tab stop marked on horizontal ruler). Toggle through the other Tabs to find Right Tab & / on Horizontal Ruler's 5 ½ inch mark (You can then / & drag the stop you just put on over to the 6" mark). Hit Tab *key* & type **Cost** (Cost is positioned to the left of your Right Align Stop mark on horizontal ruler). (Note: when you hit ® and you go to a new blank line the tab stops you set will still be there on your horizontal Ruler; so all you have to do is hit your Tab *key*)

Clear Tabs – To remove Tab stops from your page: If you wanted to remove one stop like the Center stop; simply / & drag that stop off of your Horizontal Ruler. Another quick way is Format>Tabs, /Clear All (b), /ok

Tab Leaders – Are dots, dashes or lines that track the reader's eyes from you Tab stop to the next i.e.

Books   Author   Cost

1st select ALL your lines that you want Tab Leaders in (Note: Tab Leaders are based on Tab stops, so be sure to have your Tab stops in place before inserting your Tab Leaders!), then Format>Tabs & in the big box you ought to see a list of your 2 Tab stops. Select the 1st 3" stop & under "Leader" select #2, /Set (b). Now select 2nd 6" inch stop & under "Leader" select #2, /Set (b), /ok

Clear Leaders – To clear your leaders: Select all your lines of text that have Leaders & Format>Tabs & select your 1st Tab stop 3" & under "Leader" select #1, /Set (b), /ok

Paragraph Alignment – You can have your paragraphs aligned on your document with the Alignment (b)s on Formatting *toolbar*: / in a paragraph you want aligned & on *toolbar* select your alignment (b) & /it i.e. /Left aligned (b)

Indent Markers – Up in the Horizontal Ruler on the left side are 3 small Indent Markers that can help adjust your paragraph's indentations:

First Line Indent – top triangle; when you / & drag it right, it indents 1st line of

| Mouse Click / | To > | Task Pane TP |

paragraph.

Hanging Indent – middle triangle; when you / & drag it right, it indents all but 1st line of your paragraph.

Left Indent – bottom rectangle; when you / & drag it right, it indents the whole paragraph

Borders & Shading – You can put colored borders around your text & fill-in that bordered text with a shade: Select some text you want a border around & Format>Borders & Shading, /Borders *tab* & select a Style, Color & Width & /Apply to *arrow*>your paragraph or text; Now for shade /Shading *tab* & select a color & /its Apply to *arrow*>text or paragraph, /ok (Note: Right after you apply this you can select some other text you want to apply the same formatting to & Edit>Repeat Borders & Shading)

Simple Borders – Select some text & on Formatting *toolbar* /Borders (b) *arrow*> Bottom Border or Box etc. (Note: to remove a Bottom Border (looks like a line), /above it & /Borders (b) *arrow*>No Border)

 # Lists – Used in numbering paragraphs or to create lists: On Formatting *toolbar* /Numbering (b) or Format>Bullets and Numbering

Spacing – To create spacing between your List Items or Bullets: Select your bullets & Format>Paragraph, /Indents & Spacing *tab*, under "Spacing" change "After" from 0pt>6pt, /ok

Bullets – Used to create lists or # paragraphs: Format>Bullets & Numbering

Spacing – To create spacing between your List Items or Bullets: Select your bullets & Format>Paragraph, /Indents & Spacing *tab*, under "Spacing" change "After" from 0 pt>**6pt**, /ok

Sorting – Sorting a bullet or # List. You can also sort by the field(s) in each bullet, which are created by Tab spaces (Tab spaces are the default, but you could change the "Options" to accept any punctuation marks) between text within the bullet i.e. let say in one bulleted text you typed some text, pressed the Tab *key*, typed some more & pressed Tab & finished typing. That one bullet has 3 *fields* separated by 2 Tab *key* strokes & hence there are 3 separate *fields* in that bullet you can sort by: Select all bulleted paragraphs, Table>Sort, (/Options (b) if you want to change the default from Tabs> Commas, /ok), accept default & /ok or /Sort by *arrow*>Field 1, /Then by *arrow*>Field 2 etc. & /ok…

Continuing or Restart # List – When a # List restarts, you can tell it not to, but to continue from last # & vice versa: Right /the # you want to continue (or restart)>Continue or Restart.

Outline – creating a list with a hierarchical structured to it with # or letters as main points & sub points: Select your paragraphs you want to display in an outline format & Right /it>Bullets & Numbering, /Outline # *tab*, & select an Outline Style, /ok. Now select the paragraphs you want as sub-points & on *toolbar* /Increase Indent (b) (This will demote it to a sub-letter or #)

Customize – i.e. Select your List, Right /it>Bullets & Numbering, /Customize

Button (b)	Enter or Return ®	Close X

(b), under "Level" select 3, /Number style *arrow*>Bullet or letter, /ok, /ok.

Line Spacing – For single, double or customized line spacing on your document: Select the text you want to change its spacing & on Formatting *toolbar* /the *arrow* to right of Line Spacing (b)>your choice spacing (Shortcuts: Ctrl+1, Ctrl+2, Ctrl+5 for 1.5 line spacing).

Spell & Gram Check – Right /on any misspelled word (underlined by Word with a red squiggly, or green for grammar) or on *toolbar* /Spell Check (b). If while Spell Checking you find you need to make changes, you can do it right in the Spell Check *pane*, but be sure to /Change (b) to accept your changes & for Spell Check to move to next error (Note: if Word thinks one of your words is misspelled you can Right /it>Add to Dictionary)

Thesaurus – Right /any word>Synonyms & choose one, or Right /any word>Synonyms> Thesaurus & Right /a choice>Insert

Word Count – to count up the words in your doc.: Right /any *toolbar*>Word Count *toolbar*, select some words & /Recount, or Tools>Word Count for more details, or File> Properties /Statistics *tab*

Table – Creates many cells to place and organize text in: Table>Insert>Table & type in your rows & columns, /ok, or on *toolbar* /Insert Table (b) (Note: default max of cells is a 4x5 table, but if you want more then immediately after you /Insert Table (b), then / & drag pointer over cells, past the default cells and note the little window of cells will expand to match your drag to 10x10 or more)

<u>Tab</u> – To advance from one cell to the next in your table

<u>Shift+Tab</u> – To tab backwards in your table

<u>Ctrl+Tab</u> – To actually tab in the cell without advancing to another cell

<u>Table AutoFormat</u> – To apply Word's preformatted tables to your table: 1st /inside your table & Table>Table AutoFormat & select, /ok

<u>Text to Table</u> – converting text into a table. To convert though, your text must be separated by tabs, comas or semicolons as they are the codes used to keep that text separated into their own cells when converted to a table: Select all of your text that are separated by tabs as you'd like to see them separated after converted to a table in their own cells & then Table>Convert>Text to Table, select "AutoFit to contents," & select the # of columns you expect to hold your tab separated text, /ok.

<u>Sort</u> – To sort your table: Select you table, & Table>Sort, select your options to sort by & whether you have a header row (if yes make sure that option is selected or it will sort your headings too), /ok

<u>Rearranging</u> – to move your column to another part of your table: Select a column & /Cut (b), place your cursor in another Column & /Paste (b)

<u>Sizing</u> – to change the sizes of your columns or rows: / & drag your cells top or size borders (Note: //a cells border will AutoFit it to the longest text in that Column of your table)

<u>Merge Cells</u> – To merge cells in your table: Select your cells & Right / them>Merge.

<u>Split Cells</u> – To split cells (merged or not): Right /cell>Split & select # of columns & or rows to have after it's split, /ok

| Mouse Click / | To > | Task Pane <u>TP</u> |

<u>Text Alignment</u> – aligning your text within a cell: Right /a cell>Alignment & choose (Note: you won't be able to align it in the center of the cell if that cell's borders aren't stretched out far enough)

<u>Borders & Shading</u> – Add different colored borders & shading to a cell(s): Select your cell(s), Right /it>Borders & Shading, /Borders tab & select the type of border, including thickness & color (Note: in the "Preview" / on a border to remove it & or make your changes & then /a border to apply it to one border of your 4-sided cell), /Shading tab & select a color, /ok

    <u>Invisible Table</u> – To create a table that provides layout structure to your document without the borders: Right /Your table>Borders & Shading, /Borders *tab* & under "Setting" select "None."

<u>Calculating #s</u> – You can add up columns or rows in your table: 1st find a row you'd like to add & / in a blank cell at the end of that row: Right /any *toolbar*>Tables & Borders & on *toolbar*, /Sum (b), or don't use the *toolbar* & Table>Formula, (note: sum (left), meaning all #s to left will be summed), /Number Format *arrow*>3rd choice in list, /ok. (Note: If you have more rows, after you've done the 1st row, / in the next row's Total cell & press F4 (F4 will apply the *most recent* formatting & if the last thing you did was inserting a formula, it will copy that into the cell).

    <u>Update Totals</u> – The formula's Total doesn't update automatically, you have to: Right /the cell's Total>Update or / in the cell & press F9 *key*.

<u>Chart From Table</u> – To create a chart based on your table: Select your Table, Insert> Picture, /Chart (Your chart will show along with its Datasheet)

    <u>Datasheet</u> – The #s you change in your Datasheet will update in your chart...

        <u>Close</u> – WARNING! Don't X your Datasheet by clicking its X (Close (b)), but instead // off in a blank area of your document...

        <u>Open</u> – To open your Datasheet //on your chart. (Note: If you //on the chart & your Datasheet doesn't pull up, then you did the no, no & closed your data sheet improperly, so...), / off in a blank area of your document, Right / your Chart> Chart Object>Open; when you're finished File>Exit & Return to... and now you can // on your Chart & it will pull up Datasheet!

        <u>Chart Type & Options</u> – to change your Chart's type to a pie, for example, or to add data to it i.e. values & labels: //Your Chart (Note: Chart *menu* is only available after you //the Chart, //off the Chart to properly X it)

        <u>Hide Data</u> – In the Datasheet you can hide certain parts of your Data from displaying in the chart: //Column Header (A, B, C etc.) or a Row Header (1, 2, 3 etc.), & it will make that row or column in your Datasheet faded & also hide that data from displaying in your chart. To unhide: //those Column or Row Headers again.

Table To Text – OR have you ever copied a web page into your Word document & found that they're in table format, but you'd like it in normal text? 1st select the WHOLE table & to do that / in any cell of the table & Table>Convert>Table to Text, select "Tabs" (you can select other options, but tabs works most of the time), /ok

Insert Symbols – Insert>Symbol, /Special Characters tab & select © /Insert (b) & X, or Insert>Symbol, /Symbols tab, /Font arrow>Wingdings, select a picture symbol,

Button (b)	Enter or Return ®	Close X

/Insert (b) & X.

Clip Art – to insert Microsoft's pictures: Insert>Picture>Clip Art, <u>TP</u>: /Results should be *arrow* & only check "Clip Art" & type **Halloween**, /Go (b). Find one & /it… Grab lower-right handle of your picture & / & drag it in to shrink it.

Modify Pictures –

<u>Contrast & Brightness</u> – //your picture, /Picture *tab*, change Brightness># & Contrast>#, /ok

<u>Crop</u> – to cut in a portion of your picture: On Picture *toolbar*, /Crop (b) & /on one of your Picture's border handles & drag it into the picture as far as you like … /Crop (b) again to turn it off.

<u>Lock Aspect Ratio</u> – this keeps the picture from looking distorted when you change its size to larger or smaller: //Picture, /Size *tab* & check "Lock aspect ratio" & when you enter in Height %, its Width % will match it proportionally (or / & drag the picture's handles)

Drawing Toolbar – This toolbar is used to create & edit pictures & shapes: Right /any *toolbar*> Drawing and…

<u>Text Wrapping</u> – This feature allows text to wrap around your pictures, objects & shapes, or send your shapes behind your text like a Watermark: //your picture or shape, /Layout *tab* & select "Behind Text," /ok (Note: after you / off your picture & your object is behind text, then the only way you can select that object again is on the Drawing *toolbar* / the White *arrow* "Select Objects", and then you can //your object, /Layout *tab* & select "In front of text," /ok. But you won't be able to select or edit your text until you're back to your "normal" pointer by hitting Esc *key*, or /Select Object *pointer* again to deselect it)

<u>AutoShape</u> – To create your own shapes & color them: on *toolbar* /AutoShapes (b)>Basic Shapes>any you like (Once you select it, a big annoying "Drawing Canvas" pops up to help draw your object), press Esc *key* (temporarily disables "Drawing Canvas) & /on your page & drag down & right to create your shape (Note: to permanently disable "Drawing Canvas" Tools>Options, /General *tab* & uncheck "Automatically create drawing…") /ok

<u>Order</u> – If some objects are hiding behind others and you want them in front: Select object you want in front & Right /it>Order>Bring to Front.

<u>Transparency</u> – //the shape, /Colors & Lines *tab*, type in your % in the "Transparency" *box*, /ok

<u>Color</u> – To color shapes: Select your shape & on *toolbar* /Fill (b) *arrow*>a color or "Fill Effects" (to apply a Picture, 2 colors or Gradient, Texture or Pattern to your shape)

<u>WordArt</u> – To add more visual pizzazz to a word on your document: Select your word & on Drawing *toolbar* /WordArt (b) & select a format, /ok, change its size & /ok.

<u>Add Text Box</u> – Text Boxes are mainly used to put text in a box, where you can float the box to any part on your page & add color to that box to pull focus: On *toolbar* /Text Box (b) & draw a box on your page & type in your text, /Fill Color>any light color, //Fuzzy box's border to customize your box i.e. /Layout *tab*, /Square to have the text on your page wrap around your Text Box, /ok. To move your Text

Mouse Click /	To >	Task Pane <u>TP</u>

Box, /in it first to select it, then / & drag its fuzzy border & the box will follow.

3-D Toolbar – To add 3-D effects to any of your shapes: On *toolbar*, the /3-D Style (b)>3-D Settings. Be sure to select your shape before using 3-D Setting *toolbar* to manipulate it.

Organization Chart – To create a quick Organization Chart (for more Dynamic Charts use Microsoft's Visio): On *toolbar* /Insert Diagram & Organization Chart (b), /ok. /in a shape & type in you're the **President**. To add Assistants or Subordinates, select the employee's shape & on Org *toolbar* /Insert Shape *arrow*>Assistant.

Page Watermark – To create a faded background picture or text, behind your text on each page in your document: Format>Background>Printed, select "Text Watermark," /in Text box & type **Don't Touch!** /ok (Note: follow same steps to remove Watermark too)

Margins – 1st be sure you're in Print Layout *view* (View>Print Layout. You have to be in this view to see your margins). To change all 4 margins of your document: File>Page Setup, /Margins *tab* (When finished setting your margins /Default (b) to have these settings apply permanently to all new documents & /ok)

Page Border – to place a designed border around the pages of your doc: Format>Borders & Shading, /Page Border tab, /Art *arrow*>to your choice, /Color *arrow*>any color & under "Preview" /Left border of your design (to remove it, if so desired), /ok.

Header & Footer – basically, anything you place in a header or footer will be duplicated on every page i.e. website address, company name, and you can also insert page #'s: 1st be sure you're in Print Layout *view*(View>Print Layout. You have to be in this view to see, add or edit your Headers & Footers) View>Header and Footer, scroll to the top of any page (or on Header Footer *toolbar* you can /Switch between Header & Footer (b), or you can use your Up & Down *arrow* keys to toggle between Header & Footer) & in the Header *box* or Footer, then type in some text or insert a logo you'd like duplicated in that same spot on every page (Note: on Header Footer *toolbar* /Insert Page # (b) to # your pages, or after you X out of your Header & Footer view you can Insert>Page #s as well). When finished, on the Header & Footer *toolbar* /Close (b)

Edit – Hover over faded text in Header or Footer & //it (Note: faded, but will print like normal text – faded to let you know it's not part of the original page & repeats on every page too)

Page Breaks – To insert a new page you can either:
1. Ctrl+® or
2. Insert>Break, select "Next Page" /ok (Note: This will not only insert a new blank page, but also a section break so that any page formatting you do on your new "Next Page" will not affect its previous page and visa versa!)

Page Numbering – Insert>Page Numbers, select a format, /ok

Vertical Text Align – To align you text vertically, like you could vertically center the your Title on your Title Page: File>Page Setup, /Layout *tab* & /Vertical Alignment *arrow*>Center, /ok

Organizer – Is used to copy Macros and Styles to other Documents or to the Global Template (If you copy

Button (b)	Enter or Return ®	Close X

to Global Template, then every time you open Word you will have your new Style): Tools>
Templates and Add-Ins, /Organizer (b) & select your style or macro from 1ˢᵗ little
window & /Copy (b) to add your Macro or Style over to the Global Template
window.

Section Breaks – Section breaks are inserted & used to divide or section off a page(s) layout, meaning, formatting in one section i.e. adding 3 columns, changing margins won't affect other sections of your doc. The most popular Section Break types are…

Continuous – This type is for cutting up one page into section(s) where the layout can be different in different sections of that one page: For example, to section off a 1 page document into 3 sections where Section 1 is a single column text, Section 2 is a double column text (like a newsletter), & Section 3 is single column text.

1. Place your cursor on your page in a blank line just below your Title, but above your news story text: Insert>Break, /Continuous, /ok. (The easiest way to tell if your Section Break has been applied, on *toolbar* /Show Hide (b) to seek the code. /it again to Hide those codes)
2. Next, towards the bottom of that page place your cursor in a blank line just below your news story text but above your closing title (Closing title could be: *For More Info please call…*): & Insert>Break, /Continuous & /ok
3. Now that you've sectioned your news story text off from the top & bottom of your opening & closing titles: / any where in your news story text (Note in lower-left of your window the Statistics bar. This shows "Sec 2," meaning you're currently in Section 2) & Format>Columns, /Two, /ok (Note: Your top & bottom titles are in 1 column, and only your news text that you've sectioned off is in 2 columns)

Next Page – To create a new page that is sectioned off from the other pages in your document so that any Margin adjustments or additional columns apply to that new page only: Insert> Break, /Next Page, /ok. For example, in a 5 page document you add a new page by inserting a Next Page *break* (Not only did this create a blank new page, but it also sectioned that page off from previous pages). If you change page 6's margins or add 2 or more columns, it won't apply to the previous pages. BUT the layout from page 6 will continue to affect ALL new pages, that is unless you continue to add your new pages by inserting a Next Page *break*

Columns – Once you have your page(s) appropriately sectioned off (*see Section Breaks*) you can turn your text from Word's default 1 column page into 2 or more: Format>Columns & select the # you'd like, /ok

Breaks – A Column Break prevents text from overflowing from 1 column into another: Put your cursor at the bottom of your 1ˢᵗ column & Insert>Break, /Column Break, /ok (repeat this for each column so when you add text into anyone of these columns & hit ® it doesn't affect the text in the adjacent column by rolling over your hard return & pushing that column's text down too)

Link Text Boxes – For example, Getting text from one Text Box on page 1 to continue the text, flowing over to a 2nd text box, on page 5: In Text Box 1 copy & paste all the text you want in it (don't worry if the text you place in your Text Box is too large for it, well fix that), Right /any *toolbar*>Text Box *toolbar*, /Link (b), & /inside your overflowed Text Box 1, then

| Mouse Click / | To > | Task Pane TP |

scroll to your 2nd Text Box & /in it and like magic the overflow text from Text Box 1 will continue in Text Box 2.

Macros – A macro is a recorded series of steps that you can run in a blink of a second. For example, instead of retyping your closings on various documents, record those steps & have the Macro run it for you…

Record – On Stat bar, located at bottom of window, //REC (to start recording, a *mini toolbar* pops-up) & type in a **name** for your Macro, /ok OR…

Shortcut Keys – If you'd like to run your macro with shortcut keys then /Keyboard (b) & use a combination of Ctrl, Alt or Shift *keys* for your macro i.e. hold down the Alt *key* & press Q, Alt+Q is added & the little box will say "unassigned," so it's okay to use, /Assign (b), /X (b)… OR…

Button – You can /Toolbars (b) to add it to your *toolbar*, & under "Commands" / & drag your (b) in-between some other (b)s up onto your *toolbar* above. On *toolbar* Right /your new (b)>Name & delete the extra text & leave your original name the & in the same menu go>Change Button Image> Choose a (b), /X (b) & continue with recording…

Now on your doc type **Your Full Name** ® **Your Title** ® **Your email address** ® & **Phone #** ® & on Mini *toolbar* /Stop (b) (If you accidentally closed the Mini *toolbar*, Bring up the Visual Basic *toolbar* & /its Stop (b)).

Run – To run or execute your recorded Macro on any doc: Tools>Macro>Macros & select the name of your macro & /Run (b) or use your shortcut keys Alt+Q or (b)

Edit – Editing a macro requires you understand the programming language called Visual Basic or "VB." But you can still edit & try to figure out some common sense editing techniques i.e. color = blue, you could change that statement to read color = red: Tools>Macro>Macros, select your macro & /Edit (b)

Delete – To delete a Macro: Tools>Macro>Macros, select macro, /Delete (b)

Macro (b) on Toolbar – Once you've created your macro you can add it as a (b) your toolbar: Tools>Customize, /Commands *tab*, under Categories select "Macros" & under Commands select the "name" of your macro & drag to *toolbar* like next to the Spell-check (b), In "Customize" *pane*, /Modify Selection (b) & change its name to a new **name** & Change Button Image>whatever, & be sure "Image & Text" is checked to display the name & the image ®, & /X (b).

Macro in Menu – once you created your macro you can create a custom Macro *menu* to hold your new macro(s): Right /*toolbar*>Customize, under Categories select "New Menu" & under "Commands" drag New Menu up, before Help's *menu*, in "Customize" *pane* /Modify Selection (b) & change name>**Macros** ®, then from "Categories" select Macros & drag the name of your macro> you new Macro *menu*, under the title "Macro," /Modify Selection (b) & type a **name** ® & /X (b).

MacroButton Field – is used in a document as a field (you program) with text prompting the user to type & replace your default text; hence, the user can with one / select you entire field, and type over it. For example, say your creating a form, where certain fields in your doc. You'd like the user to know what to type in that particular spot, i.e. "click here & type your full

Button (b)	Enter or Return ®	Close X

name:" Insert>Field, under "Field names" select "MacroButton," & in "Display text" type **Yo, Your name here!**, /ok. /on *field* & you can type over it (Note: Alt+F9 to reveal Field codes)

Templates – An original document you don't want changed, but where you'd like to make copies of the original to modify and save. You can also you Word's default templates if you want to send a Fax or letters…

> Use Word's Fill-in Templates – For example, File>New, <u>TP</u>: /On my computer *link*, /Letter & Faxes *tab*, //Professional Fax & fill it in…
>
> Use Word's Wizard Templates – For example, File>New, <u>TP</u>: /On my computer *link*, /Letter & Faxes *tab*, //Fax Wiz & fill out the wiz…
>
> Create Template – 1ˢᵗ create your document you want to save as your "original" or Template & File>Save As, /Save as type *arrow*>Document Template.dot, & type **name** of your Template, /Save. To extract a "copy" of your Template, File>New, & //on your Template.
>
> Delete – File>New, <u>TP</u>: /On my computer *link*, Right /your template>delete, /ok.
>
> Change Default Font – You can change Word's default font say from Times New Roman>Arial: Format>Font & select Arial, /Default (b)…
>
> Change Template Location – By default Word looks in its own Template *folder*, but you can have it look simultaneously in a folder you've created to store your own templates: Tools>Options, /File Locations *tab*, select "User Templates," /Modify & browse to find a folder you created that contains your own templates (Note: even though you've changed the default template location to your folder, funny thing, MS Word will still pull up it's default templates along with yours, and yours will appear on the "General" *tab*), /ok, /ok

Mail Merge Letters – To create a Form Letter & to address this letter to 20 different people where the only parts that change on the letter is the names & addresses etc. Before starting make sure you have
> ✓ A Form Letter and…
> ✓ A database like Excel that holds the names & address or other info that you'll later merge in certain parts on your Form Letter

Be in a new document & Tools>Letters & Mailings>Mail Merge & in <u>TP</u> "Letters" is selected,

2. /Next, select 'Start from existing doc. & /Open & find your Form Letter & //it

3. /Next, Select 'Recipients' ('Use an existing list' is selected) /Browse *link* & look for your Excel database & //it, /ok, & at this point in your <u>TP</u> you can do a few things with your Database:
> ✓ **Sort** – /Last Name column *heading* (not its *arrow*, to sort ascending or descending) and or…
> ✓ **Filter** – /State's *arrow*>Advanced: /Field *arrow*>State & in 'Compare to' *field* type **UT** (Only those clients in your Excel Database from Utah will be included in your Form Letter), /ok…

4. /Next, here you can edit your letter, Insert>Date & Time & select on, /ok & hit ® 5 times. <u>TP</u>, /Address Block, & select one, /ok®® <u>TP</u>, /Greeting Line, & select one, /ok®®

5. /Next, <u>TP</u> >> (b) to toggle through the recipients of your Form Letter (As you toggle

| Mouse Click / | To > | Task Pane <u>TP</u> |

through your recipients you can 'Exclude' some here)

6. /Next, /Save as type in a name <u>TP</u>, /Print *link* (you can choose what to what record), /Cancel. /Edit Individual Letters *link*, /ok (Your Form Letter is broken & address to each individual & you can customize each letter a little more personably...

(Note: Data sources can be from Access, Excel & Word – but in word you'd create a table and type your database in it's cells. Save it like a regular doc.)

<u>Labels</u> – To create Mailing Labels from your Excel Database: Be in a new document: Tools> Letters & Mailings>Mail Merge & in <u>TP</u> select Labels,

2. /Next, (Change Doc. Layout is selected), /Label Options *link* & select one, /ok

3. /Next, (Use An Existing Doc. is selected), /Browse *link* & find your Excel Database & //it, /ok, & at this point in your <u>TP</u> you can do a few things with your Database:

  ✓ **Sort** – /Last Name column *heading* (not its *arrow*, to sort ascending or descending) and or...

  ✓ **Filter** – /State's *arrow*>Advanced: /Field *arrow*>State & in 'Compare to' *field* type **UT** (Only those clients in your Excel Database from Utah will be included in your labels), /ok...

4. /Next, /Address block, /ok. In <u>TP</u>, under Replicate Labels /Update All Labels (b)

5. /Next,

6. /Next, <u>TP</u> /Print & note you can choose what to what record to print to, /Cancel & Save.

<u>Multiple Envelopes</u> – /New Blank Doc. (b) Tools>Letters & Mailings>Mail Merge & select Envelope

2. /Next, /Envelope Options (b) (to see default envelope size), /ok

3. /Next, /Browse, //Your Data Source.xls, /ok, & sort data by LastName *column*, /ok

4. /Next, /Show Hide (b) & /next to paragraph marker in center of envelope, / Address block, /ok. <u>TP</u> under Replicate Labels /Update All Labels (b)

5. /Next, (/Next (b) a couple of times & /Exclude this recipient)

6. /Next, <u>TP</u>, /Print & note you can choose what to what record to print to, /Cancel. /Save as **My Envelopes**... /Edit individual envelopes, /All, /ok, File>X

<u>Single Envelopes</u> – To print address on an envelope: Tools>Letters & Mailings> Envelopes & Labels, type in a Delivery address (or /Insert Address (b) if you want to use your Contacts in Outlook), & type in a Return; /on the "Feed" *picture* & select how you'll feed your envelope into the printer, /ok, then /Options (b) & check the 1st two boxes:

  ✓ Delivery Point Barcode: This prints your zip code into barcode that will process your mail a lot faster, especially if you can get the additional 4 digit zip code i.e. 84121-4452

  ✓ FIM (Facing Identification Mark): Tells the Post Office's machine which is the front-side of your letter & helps process your mail faster too...

/ok, put your envelope in the printer & /Print (b)

| Button (b) | Enter or Return ® | Close X |

Link Excel – You can insert Excel as a table, & any changes you make in your Excel Spreadsheet will automatically update: On a blank page Insert>Object, /Create From File *tab*, check Link To File *box*, /Browse & find your Excel file & //it, /ok (Excel file is now inserted as a linked table). To make changes, //the Table object to open its linked Excel workbook (Note: after making changes in Excel either save & X both Excel & Word & reopen Word, or don't close, but in Word Right /the table>update)

Chart – you can create an embedded chart in Word & Link it to your Excel's data: Select the data you want from your Excel workbook, Ctrl+C (copy it), X Excel, open your Word doc, Insert>Picture>Chart (to insert a generic chart), In the open Datasheet delete the generic data & /in 1st blank cell & Edit>Paste Link, /off your Datasheet in a blank area on you doc to X Datasheet

Closing Datasheet – WARNING! Don't close your Datasheet by clicking the X (b), but instead / off in a blank area of your document…

Open Datasheet – To open your Datasheet //on your chart. If you //on the chart & your Datasheet doesn't pull up then / off in a blank area of your document, Right /your Chart>Chart Object>Open; when you're finished File>Exit & Return to… & now you can // on your Chart & it will pull up Datasheet!

Word Outline To PowerPoint – to convert Word's text into slides, but Word must be in Outline format, and that means using Word's default Headings for styles, *see Header Styles*: /File>Send To>Microsoft Office PowerPoint (Note: how many slides are created. Heading 1 style will be the Titles for each slide).

Extract Fax Text – Microsoft's Office Doc Imaging can extract text from a scanned doc image: /Start>All Programs>Microsoft Office>Microsoft Office Tools>Microsoft Office Doc Imaging, /Open (b)>& find your .jpg .tif or .png image files & //it, /Zoom *arrow*>Text Width (to zoom in on text). / & drag to select the text & Tools>Send Text To Word, /ok, /ok (Note: the format its actually sent to, is a web page.htm, because some people don't have MS Word & Web Pages are universal, but if you do have Word then on the Web Page's *toolbar* /Edit with Microsoft Office Word (b) & it will copy the text directly into Word).

Look Up Words, Reference Books – Right /words>Look up words on the internet through References Books like dictionaries, encyclopedias etc., with result displayed in TP

Send Doc As Email – File>Send To>Mail Recipient (As Attachment)

Doc Versions – To save the current state of your doc without saving it as new file or overwriting the existing doc. The versions are always stored in the original doc: In your doc File>Versions, /Save Now & type **Original**, /ok, then make some changes in the doc & File>Versions, /Save Now & type in a name of this **Version 1**, /ok (Save as many different versions as you like). To open a previously saved version: Open the original doc the versions were saved in & File>Versions, select a version & /Open (Note: All Versions open up & the doc on the top is Original & Title Bars contain Date & Time)

Mouse Click /	To >	Task Pane TP

Delete – File>Versions, select one & /Delete, /Yes, /X

Track Changes – to track changes made to your doc without a password. This can be helpful if you send someone a letter for you to edit, and you want them to turn on "Track Changes" so it will mark ALL their changes, so after they save it and email it back to you, you can accept or reject them without trying to figure out what they changed. They can also insert comments to changes they've made to explain why: When you friend gets your doc tell them to turn on Track Changes, Tools>Track Changes (will start tracking any changes made from here on out i.e. deleting, adding text etc.). Tell them while they're changing your doc to insert comments next to those changes to explain why: Insert>Comment or /Insert Comment (b) on Reviewing *toolbar*. After they've finished tell them to /Save & email doc back to you (Note: if they forget to turn on "Track Changes" you can do it for them before you email it: *see Email Doc For Review*, or if it's too lake then see the back up plan: *see Comparing Doc*). Make some changes to doc & email it back to your friend…

> Accept or Reject Changes – When you get a doc that has been tracked & changed you can accept or reject changes with the Reviewing *toolbar*: Go to beginning of your doc & on Reviewing *toolbar* /Next & when text is highlighted /Accept (b) or /Reject (b) on *toolbar* (Note: if you have a doc where multiple users have made changes, you can turn off all except one user so you can focus on accepting or rejecting the one user & then turn the others back on to review: On Reviewing *toolbar* /Show (b)>Reviewers>& uncheck any names except one).

> Email Doc For Review – This sends out an email that turn on "Track Changes" for the other user: File>Send To>Mail Recipient (For Review) (Note: you can type numerous email addresses in the To: field, but be sure you use semi-colons as separators for each address). Then after they make their changes to your doc, tell them to /Save & Forward you back your original doc (tell them to not /Reply to your email as any attachments aren't forwarded on to the original sender).

> Doc User Information – When using the "Tracking Changes," it's important that you can track who's making the changes & they can track you. So set your User Information so that others can see your name attached to the changes you've made: Tool>Options, /User Information *tab* & type your **Name** & **Initials**.

Comparing Docs – Instead of wasting time looking back & forth between docs that are very similar do the following: Open your original Doc & Tools>Compare & Merge Documents & check Legal Blackline, (by checking this, the (b) changes from Merge>Compare so you can compare the two docs in a new doc, if left unchecked then it'll merge the changes into the 2nd doc, not the "original" or a doc you specify i.e. /Merge (b)'s *arrow*>a choice), & browse, find & //your 2nd doc (Note: New text is underlined & vertical line in left margin indicates changed lines). To accept the changes: on Reviewing *toolbar* /the *arrow* to the right of Accept Change's (b)>Accept All Changes. (Note: you can now save these changes with a new 3rd doc **name** without affecting your original & 2nd docs)

> Merge Documents – To merge one document into another & view changes: Open original doc & Tools>Compare & Merge Documents, Remove check from "Legal Blackline" if necessary & select 2nd doc, /Merge (b)'s *arrow*>any choice…

Bookmarks – To insert Bookmarks throughout the doc as a quick reference to quickly go to. For example, if you had a 20 page doc & you wanted to keep referring to a particular paragraph (Let's say a

Button (b)	Enter or Return ®	Close X

paragraph about Doughnuts!) of your doc, but you can't because that reference shifts to a different page every time you add or delete large amounts of text in your doc...

Insert – Simply / next to or select the text you want marked i.e. "Doughnut's" & Insert>Bookmark & type in a **name** & /Add (b) (Note: if won't let you /Add then you got to get rid of any spaces in your name & or odd characters).

Go To – To quickly go to a bookmark already inserted in your doc: Press F5 *key* & under "Go to what" select Bookmark, then either type in the name of your Bookmark or /Enter bookmark name's *arrow*>your name

View – To see your Bookmarks (as brackets around bookmarked text or as I beams next to unselected text): Tools>Options, /View *tab*, check "Bookmarks"

Delete – To delete bookmarks: Insert>Bookmark, select your mark & /Delete (b)

Footnote – Whenever want to make a reference or give credit to the text on a Page, you can insert a note at the foot of that page. For example, you've entered a sentence on a page that for some readers may not be clear; so insert a note at the bottom of that page referring to that sentence: / at the end of the sentence & Insert>Reference>Footnote, /Insert. You're automatically sent to the foot of the page to type in your explanation next to a reference #. (Note: After you type in your info, //its reference # & it will automatically take you back on the main page to the # being referenced to; then you can hover over that sentence's reference # & you'll see a pop-up of the text you've just entered in below as the footnote, & you can also // this # as well to go back to the bottom of the page).

Endnote – Is just like the Footnote only the reference is inserted on the very last page of your doc, not the bottom: Insert>Reference>Footnote, select Endnote, /Insert (This will automatically insert & take you to the blank page at the end of your doc with a reference #)

Captions – Used to insert text below a picture, chart, table & #'s the captions in order too: /in blank line below a picture, chart or table (Note: a quick way to scroll to your table, graphic, table or even next page: on Vertical Scroll, at it's base /the dot>table, next page etc., then /the double *arrows* above or below the dot to scroll back or forward) & /Label *arrow*>Table or Figure, & in Caption *box*, next to the bold label type **:Your Caption**, /ok

Cross-Reference – creating a cross-ref links to headings, bookmarks or captions (i.e. Figures or Tables, *see Captions*) for reader to / on to zoom right to the reference indicated by author i.e. see fig 1, fig 2 etc. For example, you've already inserted a few captions i.e. Figure 1, Figure 2 etc: Now type the text **Please see**, & / to right of "Please see" & Insert>Ref>Cross-ref, /Ref Type *arrow*>Figure 1, /Ref To *arrow*>Entire Caption, /Insert & /X (Note: if you hover over the shaded text it will prompt you to Ctrl+/ to go to Figure 1 instantly!)

Index – is an alphabetical guide to concepts in your doc appearing at end of the doc with referencing page #s for each key concept. You can manually mark the entries all your key text located in your doc or you a Concordance File...

Manual Marking Entry – to manually mark all instances of a word to later add to your index: Ctrl+F & type a key word you'd like to be in your index i.e. **Dung Beetle**, /Find Next (Note phrase is selected, very important for next step), Insert>Ref>Index & Tab, /Index *tab*, /Mark Entry (b), In Main Entry type **Bugs That Stink**, press Tab *key* & type **Dung Beatle** (Main Entry is a general index heading where you'd like

Mouse Click /	To >	Task Pane <u>TP</u>

your Subentry's to be placed or categorized under, that is if you want subentries otherwise type Dung Beetle in Main Entry), /Mark All (b), /X. (Note: On Standard *toolbar* /your Show Hide (b), because with codes on, to the right of your word "Dung Beatle" are codes. In quotes is the "Main Entry left of colon: & Subentry is at right." Also, this is where you'd edit your text, is within the "quotes").

<u>Concordance File</u> – is a file containing a two column table with specific words entered, & in the 1st column enter in what you want Word to search in your doc & in 2nd column the words you want displayed in your Index:

1. <u>Create</u> a new blank doc & insert a 2 column table with several rows according to the # of key words you'd like to appear in your index.
2. <u>Left Column</u> type in all the **key words** you want Word to look up or search & find in your doc that want inserted in your index.
3. <u>Right Column</u> type in all the **words** you want displayed in your Index. For example:

Fat	Fat
Dung Beatle	Bugs That Stink: Dung Beatle
Chicken	Meats

(Note: in 1st column, 1st cell Word will lookup "Fat" & replace that with the adjacent cell's text in column 2, "Fat." Also note, although it would make sense to have all words Word looked up replaced with the exact same words, sometimes a synonym is more appropriate. In other words, you don't have to have the same text in 2nd column. If you want to categorize your key \ words under one heading in your Index i.e. Bugs That Stink *heading* then type your Main Entry – the heading, then a colon: & a space & type your Subentry – Dung Beatle). Now save your file as **Concordance** & X it…

> <u>Index Marking</u> – After you've created your Concordance file, open the doc that has the related key words of your concordance file, that you want to insert an Index in. The next step is to mark the doc you've just opened with the key words from your concordance file: Insert>Ref>Index, /Index *tab* & /AutoMark (b) & find & //your Concordance.doc. (On *toolbar* /Show Hide Codes (b) to see the index codes throughout your doc)

>> <u>Indexing</u> – Last, but not least, once the codes have been marked it's time to insert the index itself: Go to the last blank page of your doc & Insert>Ref>Index, /Index *tab*, /Formats>Modern, Check "Right align page #s," /Modify (b), /Modify (b), /B for Bold (All Index will be bolded except Subentries), /Tab leader *arrow*> Dots, /ok

>> <u>Updates</u> – After you've marked more entries to add to your index (or deleted a code field or modified within the "quotes" of the code fields of existing entries), Right /your Index> Update & those entries will be updated.

Table of Figures or Tables – is a table that will list all Tables or Figures you've marked in your doc with a Table or Figure caption, *see Captions*: At beginning of doc Insert>Ref>Index & Tab, /Table of Fig *tab*, /Caption label *arrow*>Figures or Tables, ok.

Button (b)	Enter or Return ®	Close X

Table of Authorities – used for attorneys who have a large doc that contains court cases (also other categories are: statutes, rules, regulations etc.) – That you could say those cases are "authorities" on whatever the attorney is working on, & needs a table of those "authorities" at the beginning of the doc listing the cases throughout the doc:

Mark Entries – Select your court case (or statute, rules etc.) text i.e. **Hunchback v. Dracula, 314 US 252 (1922)** & Insert>Ref>Index & Tab, /Authorities *tab*, /Mark Citation (b), in "Short citation" *box* delete everything but "Bubba v. Dracula," /Mark All (b), /X. (Note: with show codes on, your entries that you've just marked will show field codes next to them with a code "\l" meaning long citation & "\s" is short, incase you want to edit the codes). After you've marked all your entries then go to begging of your doc & Insert>Ref>Index & Tab, /Table Authorities *tab*, /ok

Table of Contents (TOC) – Is a table that lists or references: all of Word's Heading styles you applied to your headings (*see, Header Styles*) throughout your doc, along with the page # they currently reside on. For example, Word looks for certain styles called "Headings" & if you had the name of each chapter in your doc in a "Heading 1" style, then Word can detect & copy all Heading 1's in your doc & put it on page 1 with their corresponding page #s, like indexing, but this will be a TOC. Sub-headings can also be added to TOC if the correct Heading style is added to it i.e. "Heading 2" for subs & "Heading 3" for sub-subs etc. After you have your Headings applied throughout your doc on your desired text to be copied into TOC, then create a blank page at beginning of your doc to place your TOC: Insert>Index & Tables, /Table of Contents *tab* & set Show levels>Level 1 to see only "Heading 1" in your TOC or >Level 2 to see Headings 1 & sub Heading 2, & Format *arrow*>Formal, /ok

Update TOC – After you've created your TOC & added or removed any chapters or text with their corresponding "Headings" from your doc & you want that reflected in your TOC: Right /your TOC>Update & select "Update Entire Table," /ok

Level Change – To change your TOC's levels of Headings from reading only Heading 1>include (or not include) Heading's 2 & 3: /somewhere in the middle of your TOC & Insert> Index & Tables, /Table of Contents *tab* & set "Show Levels">Level 3, /ok.

Split Window – to split your doc up into 2 windows where you can view a portion of your doc in the top window, while scrolling in the bottom to compare with top and make changes in bottom: Window> Split & /on the doc where you want to split your doc. Window>Remove Split or drag split bar to top of doc.

Master Document – holds text & links to related subdocuments. What you change in the Master will be updated in the subsdocs & what is changed in subdocs will be updated in the Master. This is great for multiple projects (docs) others are working on that need to be tracked in the Master:

1. Make sure you have all the subdocs created & ready to be inserted into the Master doc.
2. In a new blank doc (this will be saved as your Master), View>Outline View, on Outlining *toolbar* /Insert Subdocument (b) & browse & find your 1ˢᵗ subdoc & //it to insert it, and insert the rest of your subdocs (Note: the whole text of each doc inserted is fully displayed...)
3. Save your Master doc
4. On Outlining *toolbar*, /Collapse Subdoc (b) (Note: This creates a hyperlink when you hold

Ctrl & / on will open up subdoc in a separate *window*). To Expand the link on *toolbar* /Expand doc (b)

AutoSummarize – this will highlight (or copies to a new doc) certain key text or phrases in a doc that Word guesses is the most important points i.e. say someone sends you a huge doc & you don't have time to read it, but want to only browse over the most important or key points: Tools> AutoSummarize & select how you want to summarize you doc, highlighting key point etc., /ok. On AutoSummarize *toolbar* you can /arrows to increase the amount of key points for Word to highlight or decrease. To unhighlight, on AutoSummarize *toolbar* /X (b)

Doc Properties – is the place you can go to add authorship & check ownership of last doc creator, and if creator typed anything in its properties: Open a doc & File>Properties.

<u>File Search</u> – If the previous doc creator added *keywords* in docs properties on the Summary *tab* in any of its *fields*, in your Word doc File>File Search <u>TP</u>: /Advanced File Search *link*, /Property *arrow*> Keywords, & in Value *box* enter a keyword(s), or change Property *arrow*>Author or Manager & enter in Value *box* their names & /Go (b)

<u>Save Without Properties</u> – You can save your docs without your programs & computer adding "Users" name to it on the "Summary" *tab* of doc's Properties: In Doc, Tools>Options, /Security *tab* & check "Remove Personal Info…" /ok (Note: anything on the Custom *tab* won't be removed though, that you'll have to do manually).

Hide Content – you can hide anything that's selectable in a doc – incase you want readers to focus on certain parts of your doc without highlighting key text or deleting unimportant text for that given time: In your doc any text, or object & Ctrl+D, /Hidden (Shortcut is Ctrl+Shift+H), /ok (Note: Turn on your codes & see all text underline with dots, that is what is hidden when codes are turned off).

<u>Unhide</u> – The quickest way to unhide all your hidden text: Turn codes on, Ctrl+F, /More (b) (to expand Find Options), /Format (b)>Font & check "Hidden," /ok, check "Highlight all items found in" & /Find Next (b), /Cancel (b), Ctrl+D & uncheck "Hidden," /ok

Protect Parts of Doc From Changes – to prevent parts of your doc being changed by unauthorized users: Tools>Protect Doc, <u>TP</u>: check "Allow only this type of editing in the doc…" Then in doc select only the text that you don't mind others changing (or even a specified person, but to specify a person you'll have to be on a network that is hosted by a Microsoft Exchange Server) & <u>TP</u>: check "Everyone" (Note: Brackets are added around the text you've selected in your doc, signifying that part of the doc can be edited by all users, or if you're on "Exchange Server" <u>TP</u>: /More Users *link* & enter a name (check with your Network Admin for names if you don't know them), <u>TP</u>: /Yes, Start Enforcing Protection (b) & /ok & enter a password. To unprotect: Tools>Unprotect enter password (Note: if a user tries to make changes outside of what you allowed, then a note down at the bottom of Word, in Status Bar will basically tell them "they can't make changes.")

Password – Nobody can open & read your doc without a password: For example, you can put a password

Button (b)	Enter or Return ®	Close X

on a sensitive doc when you email it since emails are not always 100% safe: Tools>Options, /Security *tab* & in "Password to open" *box* type a **password** (Note: you can type a password in "password to modify" *box*; which means that anybody can open it, but they can't modify it without the password), /ok & type your **password** again to confirm, /ok. Next time when someone opens the doc they have to type in a password.

Remove – To remove password: Tools>Options, /Security *tab* & delete password
whatever is in the "password to open" *box*

Create Web Page – Webpage formats: Save your Word doc as a web page in following
formats:

- Single File Web Page (.mht or mhtml) – (default) Stores ALL related files of your doc in your web page
- Web Page (.htm or .html) – Allows use of Word's features when editing web page
- Web Page, Filtered (.htm or .html) – Use this if you won't use Word as your basic Web page editor.

Tools>Options, /General Tab, /Web Options (b) /People who view this Web page will be using *arrow*>choose one web browser version, /ok, /ok. File>Save As, /Save as type *arrow*>a Webpage format, /Change Title (b) (Title of your web page users will see on their browsers blue Title Bar when they visit it) & type a **name**, /ok & in File name type a **name**, /Save. The best way to test to see how your webpage will look is to preview it in your web browser: In your web page File>Web Page Preview.

Hyperlinks – Select some text you'd like as a hyperlink in your Web page & Insert>
Hyperlink (or Right /it>Hyperlink), /Screen Tip (b) & type in a **tip** (screen tip is when user hovers over your link this text will display), /ok, & in largest window browse & //a file you want linked to it (Note: remember that any files you link to on your computer you'll have to load them up on your Internet Service Provider's Server too)

Email – to create a link for web page viewers to /on that will open up their email with your email address in their To: field: Select the text you want as an email *link* & Right /it>Hyperlink & in Link to *section* /Email Address, & type **email@name.com** (Note: mailto: will be added to email address, but leave it as its part of the program), in Text to display type your **Name**, /Screen Tip (b) & type **Please email me**, /ok, /ok

External Links – to link your text or an object to another's website: Select your text or object & Right /it>Hyperlink & in Link to *section* /Existing File or Web Page, in Address type **www.disney.com**, /ok.

Form Fields – To create a form that can be interactive for the user to fill out electronically or on paper.
Note: when finished with the following fields: Fill-in, Text Form Field, Check Box, Drop-Down Form Field, you'll have to: /Lock (b) on Forms *toolbar* before saving & executing them
(Locking the form allows the user to only interact with the Form's *fields*, BUT you must unlock it if you want to do any editing)…

Fill-in – To open a template as a document that prompts you with questions to answer, & those answers automatically fill in parts of your doc. For example, if you want to open a Memo that prompts you to type in the name of who the memo is addressed to & put that name in a specified part of your doc: After you've created your memo, /next to your addressee's "To" *field* & Insert>Field, in Categories select "All" & in Fields

Mouse Click /	To >	Task Pane <u>TP</u>

select "Fill-in" & in Prompt type **Enter Name(s) Memo is addressed to** & then check Default Response To Prompt *box* & type its prompt *field* **Names**, /ok, /ok. (Note: Alt+F9 to toggle Fill-in codes on or off). Then save your doc as a template. To execute your prompts or Fill-in *fields*: File>New & open up your template as a doc & type in appropriate text, /ok.

<u>Text Form Field</u> – To insert these fields into the doc that when locked, & you hit the Tab *key*, it takes you to only these fields where you can quickly type in text pertinent to that field. For example, you can place a field like **Comments** at the bottom of you doc: Place your cursor at the bottom of your doc & on Forms *toolbar*, /ab| (Text Form Field) & a gray field is inserted on your doc, // it to display its properties, & in "Default Text" type **Comments**, /ok. Now lock your doc & press Tab *key* to tab to it & start typing as much text as you'd like..

<u>Check Box</u> – To add a box for you to check off with your mouse or with a pen on paper. For example, say I want to do a survey on household income to help with my marketing: On Forms *toolbar* /Check Box (b) & type **0-$29,000** & hit ® & /Check Box (b) again & type **$30,000-$5,000** i.e.

$0 - $29,000
$30,000 - $45,000

(Note: Check Boxes & other Form *fields* are shaded in gray only to help the creating process when editing your Form, and you can turn the gray off on Form *toolbar* with a / on Form Field Shading (b))

<u>Drop-Down</u> – To insert a field that when you / on drops-down & displays other choices: On Forms *toolbar* /Drop-Down (b), & on you doc // the gray *field* & type **Disneyland Trip** & hit ® then type **$3,000 cash** & hit ® & type **Mope About** & hit ®, /ok (Remember to know Lock your Form for Drop-Down to work)

<u>Save Form Data as Plain Text</u> – after you save 30 forms of client data you can save them into text that can then be imported into your database Access or Excel: File>Save As **Form Data Text**, Tools>Save Options, check "Save Data Only Form Forms," /Save, /ok (*Also see:* Excel's *Import Text File* or Access's *Import Excel*)

<u>Automate Form</u> – Say you have an 11 page doc & on page 1 you've inserted one Form *field* titled "First Name" (you obviously can insert more like an additional drop-down field for a choice of options), where the user enters the field & type his name **Bubba Gump** (or if a drop-down field, selects an option i.e. Doughnuts) & after he exits that field you'd like Word to copy & paste his name (or option selected "Doughnuts") to specific places in the rest of your doc where appropriate: After you've inserted a Form *field*, //it & change Bookmark's default, generic name to a name that makes sense like **FirstName** (Bookmarks don't like spaces or certain types of characters), then be sure to check "Calculate on exit" (so after user enters his first name & exits that field Word will update the rest of your doc with his name), /ok.

Now find a place in your doc, say next to some text you'd like the person's name to appear & Insert>Reference>Cross-Ref, /Ref Type *arrow*>Bookmark, & from list select "First Name," /Insert (b), & keep on inserting that "First Name" reference throughout the remainder part of your 10 page doc where having the persons first name is appropriate. Now on Forms *toolbar* /Lock (b), on page 1 enter your "First Name" field & type **bob**, press Tab *key* (to exit field so Word can update the doc. Note: you can Alt+F9 to view reference codes throughout your

Button (b)	Enter or Return ®	Close X

doc to delete them or modify them).

IF Function – After you've appropriately named your Form *field's* bookmarks in the step above, you can use an IF Function to decide what AutoText to insert (or text, but please *see AutoText* if you don't know anything about his feature), depending on what the user types in a Form *field* (or selects if a drop-down Form *field* is used). For example, say you have a drop-down Form *field* named "Work Party Choices," (with it's bookmark name "Party") with the choices Pizza, Doughnut and Grapefruit, you could for each item selected, have some text to add to your doc or letter about it i.e. the user selects "Grapefruit," you could then insert an IF *function* code on a page of your doc or letter you choose to insert the AutoText "While you chose grapefruit to have at our work's party next Saturday, a healthy drink, the taste is nasty without a lot of sugar and so bring your own." (Note: to turn the grapefruit paragraph into AutoText, first type your paragraph, then select it & Insert>AutoText>New & type the name of your text **grapefruit,** /ok. Repeat this step to create AutoText for Pizza & Doughnut). Find a spot on your doc to insert specified AutoText a user has selected from the "Work Party Choices" drop-down *field* &: Insert>Field, /Categories *arrow*> Document Automation, & select "If" *function*, /Options (b), select a bookmark (bookmark you name your "Work Party Choices" *field* with), /Add to Field, /ok, /ok, turn on the codes Alt+F9 & then edit what code you do see to look like this:

{ IF { REF Party * MERGEFORMAT } = "Grapefruit" "{ AUTOTEXT Grapefruit * MERGEFORMAT } " * MERGEFORMAT }

IF Syntax or basic meaning: IF{Party *bookmark*} = "a 'selection' from a drop-down *arrow* field or specific 'text' in a Text Box field" {"then insert the AutoText 'Grapefruit'"}

Or, if you prefer not to use AutoText, as too many key words in your AutoText can drive the typist crazy with all those pop-ups, then look at the following example to re-code your MERGEFORMAT codes accordingly (Note: this example is best used only on Text Box *field*, not drop-down *arrow* Form *field*):

{ IF { REF Party * MERGEFORMAT } = "Pizza" "Congrats on choosing pizza!" "Why didn't you choose pizza? You know your boss only likes pizza at parties. You're fired!" * MERGEFORMAT }

IF Syntax or basic meaning: IF{Party *bookmark*} = "Pizza" then display "Congrats on choosing pizza!" if not then display "Why didn't you choose pizza? You know your boss only likes pizza at parties. You're fired!" (Note: Alt+F9 again to hide merge *fields*).

Print Doc Check Box – You can add a check box that when entered & checked will print out pages 2-11 of your doc, as page one is the form that you may not want printed. First create the macro that will print specified pages 2-11: At bottom of Word, in middle of Status Bar, //REC (it's very faded, but when //will start recording process), type in name of your macro **Print** (Note: Macros don't like spaces in their names & other certain characters), /ok. File>Print, enter the pages you want printed **2-11**, & /Print (b), after it's printed then /Stop (b) on your floating Macro *toolbar*. Next, on your form, from Forms *toolbar*, add a Text Box *field* to your form, //that gray *field* (to bring up its properties), & /Entry *arrow*>**Print**, /ok. Next to that check box you may want to type something like After you fill out the form, check this box

| Mouse Click / | To > | Task Pane TP |

to print out the rest of the pages. (Remember to Lock Form to have this work)

Book Fold – Used to set your doc up to print out like a book, pamphlet, newsletter etc.: File>Page Setup /Multiple Pages *arrow*>Book Fold (Note: changes wording of right & left margins> inside & out)

> Gutter – Adds extra room for inside margins on both left & right pages for binding. If you want extra room for your inside outside margins for book binding: File>Page Setup & type amount of desired Gutter in Gutter *field* i.e. .5, /ok

> Odd/Even Headers – Like a book you can have titles for all the odd pages ("Chapter #") different or separate from all the even pages ("Chapter Name"): File>Page Setup, /Layout *tab* & check "Diff Odd & Even" & "Diff 1st Page," /ok. View>HeaderFooter & scroll>header of 2nd page & type "Your Name" (as the author), then scroll down to page 3's header & type "Name of your Book." File>Print Preview to see what it will print out like

> Print Book – Once you have your Multiple Pages set up>Book Fold it's important to print correctly too. Though every printer is different here's a general way to print your book: 1st be sure to Insert page #s (Insert>Page #s) & then Ctrl+P, /Properties (b) & /Features or Advanced *tab* & look for "Two Sided Printing" & check it & uncheck "Automatic" (On some print jobs if you don't uncheck this the printer won't prompt you on your computer after it has printed one side of your book to FLIP printed pages over & insert them back into your printer so it can print the other side), & /ok, /ok

Shortcuts

Alt+Tab – Use this key combo when you have more than one program and you want to "alternate" or "switch" *fast* between your programs (Note: after you hold Alt *key* down & press Tab *key* once a little window opens and will take you to your most "recently" viewed program, BUT if you have more than two programs open, press Tab *key* a couple of times with Alt *key* held down & you'll be able to toggle to other programs that are open)

F4 – Like Format Painter, *but* it only applies *most recent* action or format performed.

Ctrl+Home – Puts cursor at the very beginning of the document.

Ctrl+End – Puts cursor at the very end of the document.

Home – Puts cursor at beginning of a line.

End – Puts cursor at end of line.

Ctrl+A – Selects *all* text in document.

Ctrl+Z – Undo any action

Ctrl+Y – Redo any undid action.

Ctrl+1 – Single space

Ctrl+2 – Double space

Ctrl+5 – 1 ½ spacing

Ctrl+T – Hanging Indent

Ctrl+S – *Save*

Ctrl+X – *Cut*

Ctrl+C – *Copy*

Ctrl+V – *Paste*

Button (b)	Enter or Return ®	Close X

Dream Notes 2003

<u>Ctrl+F</u> – *Find*
<u>Ctrl+H</u> – *Replace*
<u>Ctrl+P</u> – *Print*
<u>Ctrl+D</u> – *Font*

Mouse Click /	To >	Task Pane <u>TP</u>

Excel

Editing Cell – // the cell you want to edit its #'s or text, or / in cell & then / up in Formula *bar* & edit. Press Esc *key* to exit editing.

Inserting Columns & Rows – Right /on a row (1, 2, 3 etc.) or column (A, B, C etc.) *header>* Insert or delete.

Inserting Cells – Select a range of cells & Right /them>Insert (Shifts cells selected down or right) or delete (deletes selection & them pulls other cells into its deleted range up or left).

Selecting Cells – To select a group of cell, sporadically hold Ctrl *key*, to select in blocks hold Shift *key*

Save – When you save your spreadsheet for the 1ˢᵗ time Excel performs a Save As! But after you save it once all you have to do is on *toolbar* /Save (b) & it will save without any questions.

Save As – When a spreadsheet is saved for the 1ˢᵗ time Excel will open a small window to ask you a couple of questions before it can save your spreadsheet:
1. <u>Where</u> do you want to save your document: /Save in *arrow>*a place like a *folder* or your Desktop
2. <u>What</u> is the name of your document: In File Name *box* type in the **name** of your document & /Save

Also, if you have a spreadsheet saved to Sam & you want to create a copy for Cathy without having to retype it: File>Save As & rename the File **Cathy**. Now you'll have 2 spreadsheets: 1 for Sam & 1 for Cathy

Copy or Move Data – To move or copy data from 1 cell to another:
- Select the cell & on *toolbar* /Cut (b) or /Copy (b) & then / in a different cell & on *toolbar* /Paste (b) (Press ESC *key* to get rid of marching ants), or after you copy a cell Edit>Paste Special & select an option like "Formats" and it will on paste the Format of what you copied OR,
- / the cell's border & drag, or hold Ctrl & / & drag the cell's border to make a copy of that cell.

Back Ground Picture – Format>Sheet>Background & browse to find & //a Picture. To delete: Format>Sheet>Delete Background

AutoFill – Or the black cross +, used to repeat a cell or a range of cells' patterns i.e. if you have 5 columns of data to add up, first use a function or create a formula to add up column one and: Move mouse over lower-right corner of that cell until you see your pointer change to a black cross +, then drag / & drag that cross right & it will copy the formula, not the values, from your first cell into each successive cell you drag the AutoFill handle to (Note: drag AutoFill right to fill up columns of data or down to for rows of data. Also, you can even select a

Button (b)	Enter or Return ®	Close X

range of cells and drag the lower-right corner cell of that selected range right or down to repeat the selected data).

Find & Replace – To find & or replace text or numbers in a cell: Edit>Find & type in what it is you want to find & /Find Next. If you need to find certain formatted cell or text with certain styles Edit>Find & type in your #s or text & then /Options (b) & /Format (b) & select a particular format to those #s or text you're trying to find & /Find Next. For find & replace type in what you're finding & /Replace *tab* & type in what you want it replaced with including any special Format (Warning! Once set the Format (b) to find a certain format, the Format will not clear after you find it; so if you want to find something else /the arrow to right of Format's (b)>Clear Format)

Spell Check – Press F7 *key*

Text to Speech – Excel can read back your cells' data to you: 1st select a range of cells you want read back to you, then in menu View>Toolbars>Text To Speech & on the toolbar press Play (b).

Formulas – always begins with typing = i.e. =d3+d4+d5
=**max(A5:B6)** (this formula finds the highest # in range A5 through B6)
=**min(A5:B6)** (this finds the lowest # in the range)
=**count(A5:B6)** (this counts up the # of cell in the range)
=**sum(A5:B6)** (this adds us the range)

Functions – are pre-set formulas where the user only enters the values or cells to be affected or used in the function i.e. you want to add up cells A1:A10: / in A11 & up on Formula Bar /Insert Function (b) fx & //Sum, /the first Red arrow (b) (window collapses to allow you to select your range of cells) & select A1:A10 & hit ® ®.
Editing – Note if you // any cell with a formula or function in it, Excel will outline it precedents or values in a blue box that you can then / & drag the blue borders to lasso more or less #s in your formula.

PMT – To calculate payments on a loan, to set up: assign 3 cells to contain "Interest" (say A5), another cell assigned for "# of payments" to be made (say A6), and assign the "Total" of the loan (say A7). / in a cell to figure the 3 variables (say A8) & /f(x) (b), /Or select a category *arrow*>Financial & select PMT *function*, /ok. In first *field* enter interest rate **A5/12** (A5 is Divided by 12 months), 2nd field enter # of payments **A6**, 3rd field enter total loan **A7**, ®. (Note: now you can change cells A5-A7 with different #'s, that will result with different monthly payments in A8)

VLOOKUP – Vertical Lookup; to lookup up a value in a table and return its compliment value. Syntax: vlookup (<u>what</u> to lookup, <u>where</u> to look it up like a table (it will look in table's left most column & check if it's greater than the *what*), <u>which</u> column # contains desired info). If *what* you're looking up is greater than the values in the *where* (table's left most column) you're looking up, then it will return the value in same row from a column you

Mouse Click /	To >	Task Pane <u>TP</u>

specified. (Note: good example is your IRS taxable income: look up in tax table to return value or tax owed from 2nd column Single or 3rd column Married etc.):

1. Create a two column table (or more) with many rows, and in its 1st row (the dead row) type in your column **headings** & below the dead row in the left column type your **totals** you'd like later compared & in right column type in the **values** you'd like returned from your lookup. Select all the cells in your table (except the dead row) & in up *toolbar* in Namebox type a name for your table & hit ®.
2. /in an cell, adjacent to another cell that has a # in it you'd like to look up & compared to in your new table, then on *toolbar* /fx (b) & /Or select a category *arrow*>Lookup & under "Select a function" select VLOOKUP, ®…Type the **cells reference** i.e. A4, you want compared to your table, press *tab* & type in **name of your table** (or range of your table i.e. A5:B7), press *tab* and type in the **column #** you want to retrieve the data, (Note: you could use the Last *field* "Range Lookup" to type **False**, and it will bring back only exact matches; in other words, the lookup has to match the number in the left most column of the table, otherwise it displays N/A), ®.

Randomize – using the "Data Analysis" Add-in to capture a random sample (numeric data only) from your database: Tools>Add Ins & check "Data Analysis," /ok. Tools>Data Analysis, select "Sampling," ®, /Input Range's Collapse (b) & select your range of data you want to pull a random sample from i.e. A5:A50 ® & in "Number of Samples" type the # of random samples you want pulled from your list of 45 i.e. **5**, under "Output options" select "New Worksheet" & type in its **name** in adjacent box "Group Sample," /ok (Note: You can only pull #'s, not text, but after you've pulled the #s you can pull their corresponding labels if any by using the VLOOKUP *formula, see VLOOKUP*).

DSUM – This function adds up #s of duplicate labels scattered throughout a *column* of your database, based upon criteria you create in a subdatabase. Syntax: dsum (database range, column header name, mini criteria database) i.e. We have 3 columns in our "Candy" database (1st column is labeled "Candy"), 2nd flavors & 3rd is Retail. We want to find out store's Retail cost on the candy Nerds & Gummy Bears (Note: Nerds can be listed several times, because it has many flavors, and we want the total retail of ALL Nerds & Gummy Bears). First create your little subdatabase by finding an empty cell in *row* 1 (say cell F1. Note: by default Excel always sees *row* 1 as a *heading row* & doesn't need to be formatted in order for Excel to distinguish it from the rest of the data entered below it), & type in the *heading* **Candy** (Note: this heading in our subdatabase has to match the heading "Candy" in our main database so later Excel can compare the "Main" with the "Sub"), & type below that *heading* what you want filtered out of the main database for that heading i.e. **Nerds** and type below it **Gummy Bears**. When finished /in a blank cell & /fx (b) & select DSUM *function* & hit ®, & in first box type the **range** of your Candy *database* & include their *headers*, press Tab *key* & type in "quotes" the name of one of the column labels in your database you want to the DSUM to search and add up i.e. **"retail"**, press Tab *key* & type the **range** of your criteria subdatabase i.e. **F1:F3** ® (Note: you now get the retail totals of all flavors of: Nerds & Gummy Bears)

IF – a calculated test, & if true you can program it to display one thing or if false programmed to display something else. Syntax for function is IF(logical_test, value_if_true, value_if_false): /in a blank cell & on *toolbar* /fx (b) & /Or select a category *arrow*>Logical & select

Button (b)	Enter or Return ®	Close X

"IF", ®. In top *field* type in a "Logical test" i.e. A6>=33 (the test is whatever is in cell A6 has to be greater than or equal to 33), press Tab *key* & type what you want if its true, i.e. A6*22% (for true, you said to multiply whatever is in cell A6 by 22%), press Tab *key* & type in **0** or in quotes **"You are soo Fired!"** (for false, you said that if cell A6 is not greater than 33, then either 0 bonus or they get "Fired!")

Nested IF – an example of a nested if function for figuring a student's letter grade:

=IF(A2>89,"A",IF(A2>79,"B", IF(A2>69,"C", IF(A2>59, "D", "F"))))

Now – A function used to always enter in today's date every time you open Excel: / in a cell you always want to show today's day & type **=now()** ® (Enters current date & time)

AutoSum (b) – For quick sum of cells. Note the little *arrow* to right of AutoSum (b) on your toolbar, /its arrow>get quick calculations on other Functions i.e. Average, Max etc.: / in a blank cell adjacent to the range of cells you want to add & on *toolbar* & /AutoSum (b) on *toolbar*, make sure the marching ants select your range you want summed, if not use mouse to / & drag your new selection of cells & hit ®

Absolute References – Prevents a reference from changing when you copy & paste the formula of 1 cell into another i.e. if you have one cell that will be divided by all the rest, that "one cell" is a constant & you want that once cell's reference to *stay!* Before you copy or AutoFill the formula to another cell, up in Formula Bar, place cursor before cell reference you want to *stay* & press F4 (it will add $ or Absolute Values to your formula. Easy way to remember this is Fido! When you want to tell your dog Fido to stay or in this case a cell called an "Absolute Reference" there are **4** letters in Fido & it begins with the letter **F, F4**!)

Adjusting Rows & Columns Size – Right /a Row or Column *header* i.e. A, B, C or 1, 2, 3 etc.>Format Column or Row   Width & type in a #, ®

Hide Rows & Columns – The rows or columns you hide also won't print either: Select a row(s) & Right /it>Hide. To unhide select the Row before and after the hidden row i.e. if you hid row 3, then select rows 2 & 4, Right that selection>Unhide.

Merge Cells – Select range & up in *toolbar* /Merge & Center (b) or Right /your selected range>Format Cells, /Alignment *tab* & check Merge cells (Note: here you can also select the merged cells alignment by /Horizontal *arrow*>Top, bottom or center & Vertical's *arrow* too!)

Unmerge – select merge cells & /Merge & Center (b) again

Wrap Text – After merging cells together you can have the text wrapped from top to bottom of the merged cells by: Right /cell>Format Cells, /Alignment *tab* & check "Wrap text," /ok

Formatting Cells – Changing the cells color, font, # style, border (to outline a cell in color), or alignment: Right /cell>Format cells.

Custom Format – Right /cell(s)>Formatting cells, /Number *tab* & select Custom, / in Type *field* & use quote marks "" around the text you want as a part of your

| Mouse Click / | To > | Task Pane TP |

format i.e. "SS" for Social Security, /ok. You can then drag the AutoFill handle of that cell down to the remaining cells you want to apply its same formatting too & then /the Smart Tag's *arrow*>Fill Formatting Only.

Clear Formats – Edit>Clear>All

Custom # Formats – to customize a cell's #'s: Right /a cell>Format Cells, /Number *tab* & select "Custom," scroll down & choose a complicated #format & in Type: *box* edit the format to produce certain characteristics i.e. the following Custom format is divided into 4 sections, each section is separated by a semi-colon:

_(* #,##0.00_);_(* (#,##0.00);_(* "-"??_);_(@_)

Section 1 – Positive numbers

Section 2 – Negative numbers

Section 3 – Zeros

Section 4 – Text (to always display text; put them in "quotes")

Codes –

0 = to make numbers visible

0.00 = not only displays whole numbers, but also 2 numbers after the decimal.

= when # used with 0, the desired result is to display larger numbers like in the thousands with commas i.e. #,##0 (Note: remember you have to have at least one 0 to make your numbers visible)

@ = the text the user types in (keeps the user's text & makes it visible. Note: if you place text in "quotes" before the @ symbol then that text will always show up and precede, in addition, to what ever the user types in).

[blue] = place any set of brackets with one of the following colors typed in them, at the beginning of each section to color code that section: black, magenta, white, green, yellow, cyan & red.

_ = underscore outside the 1st parenthesis, but inside the 2nd prevents the parenthesis from showing.

* = closes the gap or spacing between a symbol & a number.

? = spaces.

Example of Custom Format –

_(+$* #,##0.00_);[red]_(-$* (#,##0.00);[magenta]_(* "Null"??_);[Cyan]_(@_)

Section 1 – All positive numbers will precede with a + and $ signs

Section 2 – All negatives will precede with – and $ signs, and colored red

Section 3 – Any zeroes will be replaced with the text Null in Magenta

Section 4 – Any text entered will be colored cyan

Style – To save a format style. Select the cell with the style in it you want to save &: Format>Style & type in Style Name *box* a **name**, /ok. To apply style, Format>Style & /Style Name box *arrow*>your **named** style, /ok.

Cell Borders – To outline a cell with a black border. *Toolbar*, /the *arrow* on right-side of the Border (b)>Thick Box Border, or Right /Cell>Format Cells, /Border *tab*, /Outline (b), /ok.

Button (b)	Enter or Return ®	Close X

AutoFormat – applying a template format to you cells: Select your range of cells, Format> AutoFormat & select, /ok

Manipulating Worksheets – To manipulate the worksheets…

<u>Sheet Tabs</u> – Delete, Insert, color, move, copy or rename worksheets: Right /worksheet *tab*.

<u>Moving Sheet(s)</u> – To change orders of worksheets: / & drag the sheet tab before or after another tab, or to move to a new Workbook: using Shift *key* select several Sheets & Right /selected>Move or Copy, /To *arrow*>New Book & check "Create a copy," /ok

<u>Copy Sheet</u> – To duplicate a worksheet: Hold Ctrl, / & drag that sheet's *tab* before or behind an adjacent worksheet *tab*

Freeze – You can freeze rows or columns or both at same time…

<u>Rows</u> – To keep a fixed set of rows frozen when you scroll down your spreadsheet: / below the row you want frozen but must be in A *column*, then in *menu* Window>Freeze Panes…

<u>Unfreeze</u> – Window>Unfreeze (Note: whatever cell you select everything will freeze above & to the left of it).

<u>Columns</u> – To keep a fixed set of columns frozen when you scroll right in your spreadsheet: / after the column you want frozen but keep it in 1 *row*, then in *menu* Window> Freeze Panes

(Note: whatever cell you select everything will freeze above & to the left of it).

Print Titles – To have a select set of rows printed on each sheet: File>Page Setup, /Sheet *tab* & /Collapse (b) for "Rows to repeat at top" & select your Rows (Note: rows can only be selected as a group, not sporadically here & there), /ok

Headers Footers – To put text, pictures, page #'s, dates in the headings or footings of each printable sheet. View>Header and Footer & /Customer Header or Footer (b) & type in what you'd like in 1 of 3 *sections*

Margins – to change printable margin settings: File>Page Setup, /Margins *tab*

Page Break – If your sheet isn't fitting correctly in your print preview: In Print Preview, /Page Break Preview (b) on *toolbar*, then find & / & drag your dark, dashed, blue page break line on the page to where you want page to break. When finished, to get back to normal view, *menu* View>Normal (Note: You can insert a page break manually in your spreadsheet: Insert>Page Break, but to remove it you have to have the cell selected AFTER the dotted page break line in your spreadsheet, otherwise you won't see Remove Page Break in the Insert *menu*)

Print Range – Prints an area specified. Select the range of cells you want printed, File>Print Area>Set Print Area (To Clear Print Area: File>Print>Clear Print Area)

Split – To split your spreadsheet into separate windows, so you can view one part of your sheet, and scroll to another part in the other windows: select a key cell where you want to divide your spreadsheet at, Window>Split. You can / & drag the bars inserted around, or to the margins of the spreadsheet to remove one or both bars, or Window>Remove Split.

Arrange Worksheets – it's like Split Window, but it creates a temporary copy(s) of your workbook instead, so you can have many views to look at of your same workbook: Window>New Window, Window>Arrange & select an options like "Horizontal," (Note: you can now see that the second Workbook's Title Bar is the same title but adds the # 2, you can continue to Window>New Window to add more views of your same Workbook, but you can't save the temporary copies, nor can you X your original Workbook first, but you'll have to X all the open temporary copies first.)

Hiding Sheets – to hide worksheet(s) from temporary prying eyes or to keep other users focus on what's not hidden: Select a worksheet or use Shift *key* & select many, Format>Sheet>Hide. To unhide: Format>Sheet>Unhide…

Quick Calculations – To see a quick summary or average of selected cells, use the Status bar: 1st Select a range of cells, then down at the bottom, right side of your spreadsheet, Right /on Status bar>Sum or whatever it is you want a quick calculation of.

Templates – To save your creation into an original that can't be directly edited, but only copies of it can be made: File>Save as & /Save as type *arrow*>Template (*.xlt), type in a file **name** & /Save. To open a template or to view some of Excel's own templates i.e. Sales Invoice: File>New, TP: /On my computer *link*, find your template & //it or /Spreadsheet Solutions *tab*, //Sales Invoice (Note: Opening a template actually only opens a copy of it, so when you save, its "type" will default as a "Workbook," but if you want to make changes and overwrite your template save it as a Template (*.xlt) "type" with the same name)
Delete – File>New, TP: /On my computer *link*, find your template & Right /it> Delete.
Online Templates – Excel has more templates online you can use: File>New, TP: in "Search online for" *box* type **statements**, /Go & it will pull up (currently) all 30 Excel templates you can download & use.

Online Thesaurus & Dictionary – Right /a cell with a single word in it>Look up, TP: scroll down in largest *window* to find a Thesaurus, then find the word you want to replace & /its *arrow*>Insert, or expand the other options like Dictionary (Note: if you have a cell containing many words, //that cell, //the word, Right /that word>Look up & hit ®)

Cell Comments – Adding comments to a cell that pop up when you hover your mouse over them: Right /any cell>Insert Comment & type in your comment & when finished /in a blank cell. To Edit comments: Right /cell will comment>Edit. To Delete comments: Right/cell>Delete

Hyperlinks – to link your workbook to any other file: Right /any cell you want linked to another application or workbook>Hyperlink, browse & find a file to //. To edit Links Name: Right /Linked *cell*>Edit Hyperlink
Email Link – Right /any cell>Hyperlink & /Email Address & type in your **email address**, /ok

Button (b)	Enter or Return ®	Close X	

Charts – To create a chart: 1ˢᵗ select your data & on *toolbar* /Chart Wizard (b), select a chart "type," /Next, /Series *tab* & under "Series" select "Series 1" & in Name *box* type a **name** to rename "Series 1" & repeat renaming with any remaining successive "Series #s," /Category (x) axis label's Collapse (b) & select the corresponding labels of your chart data (if any) & hit ®, /Next & type in your chart's title name and other options, /Next & select an embedded chart on giving the chart it's own worksheet, /Finish

Options – Add a legend, labels or axis titles: Chart>Chart Options. (Note: Make sure your "embedded" chart is selected otherwise there will be no "Chart" *menu*)

Types – Change current chart into another i.e. column to pie: Select Chart & Chart>Chart Type…

Organization – A chart that outlines your company's employee hierarchy: Insert>Diagram& select the top box and type in the President of the company's name, use Tab *key* to tab from box to box to type in the rest of the employees. To insert coworkers, or assistants to a box: select the box & on Organization Chart *toolbar* /Insert Shape (b)'s *arrow*>coworker.

Format Chart – Right /fuzzy border of org chart>Format Organization Chart…

Chart Trend Line – a line marking a trend in the chart, to predict future Trends. Note: the chart you create must have points for the trend line to apply or follow: Right /chart points or dots>Add Trend line, /Options *tab* & change Forward>**2** (to set trend out, to forecast the trend by 2 points), /ok

Drawing Toolbar – Used to insert Clip Art, create & manage objects. To bring up Drawing Toolbar, Right /any (b) on your current *toolbar*>Drawing:

Clip Art – Microsoft pictures you can use: /Insert Clip Art (b),

TP: in "Search for" type a name of a category i.e. Halloween & /Go (b)… Scroll the pictures listed and Right /it>Insert

Rotate – to rotate your picture: /on your inserted Clip Art, at it's top / & drag the green dot left or right…

Crop – to cut back the sides of the picture: On Picture's *toolbar*, /Crop (b), then / & drag one of the thick border dashes or triangles surrounding your picture & in to the picture as far as you want to cut it back, & pres ESC *key* to exit.

Circles & Squares – to create circles & squares: /on Oval (or Rectangle), hold SHIFT *key*, / & drag. To create multiple circles, //Oval… when finished hit ESC *key*.

Center Objects – To center an object within another object: / on 1ˢᵗ object, then hold SHIFT & /on remaining object to be aligned, /Draw>Align or Distribute>Align Center then go back & repeat>Align Middle.

Send To Back – To send an object on top of another, behind it: Select top object, /Draw>Order>Send to back.

Selecting Objects – To select objects if original mouse pointer doesn't work: On Drawing *toolbar* /White Arrow & then you can select object, but to go back to selecting text or cells again hit ESC *key*.

Group – to group objects together i.e. you have two circles you can group them as one:

Select the 2 circles using the Shift *key* & on Drawing *toolbar* /Draw> Group

Create Name Ranges – To give a cell or a range of cells a name. Note: if you rename cell A5 to "Bonus" it can be referred to in a formula as A5 or Bonus, also that name can be also be referred to from another worksheet or workbook. Or you can name a range of cells i.e. "EEHours," and you can create a formula that will add up all the cells in the named employee hours range i.e. =sum (eehours): Select a cell or a range & up in "Name Box" (left of Formula bar) /in it & type in a new **name** (with no spaces & maximum of 12 characters) & hit ® (Note: another feature is after you create your name: /in a blank area and then /Name Box's *arrow*>the name and it will take you to it and select the cell or range you named).

<u>Delete Named Cell or Range</u> – Insert>Name>Define & select the name & /Delete

Link Data – Pulling data from one worksheet (or workbook) and linking it in another; so when you change data in one worksheet it updates in the other(s) cell or formula that data is a part of: /in a blank cell and type = then /on worksheet B and select a cell that has some data & hit ® & any change you make in that cell on worksheet B will up date in worksheet A. Formulas work same way i.e. in worksheet A /in a blank cell and type **=sum(** Then / on worksheet B and using the Ctrl *key* select multiple cells you'd like to add to your SUM *formula* & when done hit ®, again any changes you make on worksheet B that is linked (using the equals sign links them), will update in your formula on worksheet A.

Sorting – To sort data ascending (A to Z) or descending (Z to A): /in column you want sorted & up on toolbar /A – Z or Z – A.

<u>Multilevel</u> – To sort more than one column: Menu Data>Sort

<u>Consecutive Sorts</u> – Allows you to sort your lists by more than 3 columns. Sort the least important *columns* 1st & then sort again i.e. to Sort 5 *columns*: Data>Sort & use all 3 Sort fields & then repeat; Data>Sort & use 2 Sort fields.

<u>Months</u> – Months by default are sorted by Excel as Apr, Aug, Dec etc., but to sort months as Jan, Feb, Mar etc.: /inside Month *column* & Data>Sort, /Options (b), /First key sort order *arrow*>January, February, March, April (Note: if your months are abbreviated as Jan, Feb, Mar. etc. then /First key sort order *arrow*>Jan, Feb, Mar., otherwise it won't work, formatting must be kept same)

AutoFilter – To have column headers display drop-down arrows that can be used to filter your database: / in a cell in your Database & Data>Filter>AutoFilter. To clear Filtered *columns* to re-filter: Data>Filter>Show All. To remove AutoFilter: Data>Filter>AutoFilter

<u>Wild Card</u> – To use * to help filter a column i.e. if you want all last names that begin with the letter D*: / the column's *header* filter arrow>Custom & /in the box to the right of "Equals" & type in a wild card **D***, /ok (asterisks means anything, hence show all name that begin with letter D, but doesn't matter what comes after it)

Advance Filter – To create a subdatabase off to the side of your original database that has a list of what you'd like to see filtered out of your original: Create you little subdatabase by 1st typing in

Button (b)	Enter or Return ®	Close X

the **headings** that match those in the main database on row A (by default Excel always sees row A as a *heading* row & doesn't need to be formatted specially in order for Excel to distinguish it from the rest of the info typed in below it), & type below your heading what you want filtered out of the main database for that heading. When finished /anywhere in the middle of your main database & Data>Filter>Advanced Filter, /Criteria range's collapse (b) (little red arrow) & select the range of your subdatabase (select all of the subdatabase including its *headings*), hit ® (pops open collapsed window), hit ®. To undo Filter: Data>Filter>Show All

Subtotals – To subtotal a specified column(s) that has been previously sorted ascending (A to Z). If there is any duplicate data in that column (or groups), then you can subtotal those groups: Data> Subtotals, /At each change in *arrow*>"the name of your column" you have duplicates in, ®. To Remove: Data>Subtotals, /Remove All

Exporting – exporting Excel in other formats incase another computer doesn't have Excel so user can view your Excel's data:

XML – has numerous application use, but basically for web use: /Save as, /Save as type *arrow*>XML Spreadsheet

CSV – Comma delimited used for databases: /Save as, /Save as type *arrow*>CSV (Comma delimited)

Text – Tab delimited used for word processing: /Save as, /Save as type *arrow*>Text (Tab delimited)

HTML – For web pages and viewing on web: Select a worksheet you want as a webpage & File>Save as Web Page, /Change Title (b) & type a **title** for your webpage, select "Selection Sheet," & check "Add interactivity," & type a **name** for you file in File Name *box*, /Publish, check "AutoRepublish," /Publish. Your webpage will be a .htm file saved in the folder you published it in.

Word – File>Save as & /File Type *arrow*>Tab Delimited, /Save, /ok, /Yes & File>X, /No. Open Word & File>Open, /File Type *arrow*>All, //Export.txt

Importing – importing other programs into Excel:

Web – To import tables into Excel from Internet: Data>Import External Data>New Web Query & type in desired web site address. /A *yellow tag* to select a table, /Import (b), /any cell to import your data ®

Refresh – To refresh imported data from web: 1st /in cell where you imported your data & on External Data *toolbar* /Refresh (b)

Access – Data>Get External Data>New Database Query, & select MS Access Database ® & select your database ® From Available *list* select a table & /the right add arrow (b), /Next, /Next, /Finish… /ok.

Word Table – Open your Word document that has your table in it & Table>Select> Table, /Copy (b). In Excel, /Paste (b)

Text File – importing files exported into text from another program: In Excel, File>Open the.txt *file*, /Next & check a delimiter (Note: when a file is exported from another program the exporter will tell the file to keep its data separated by delimiters i.e. Tabs, commas or semicolons so when you import it into Excel the data won't be all bunched up into on cell but separated by those delimiters, so ask the person what delimiter was used in their exporting), /Next, /Next, /Finish.

Creating Database – To sort effectively & correctly, there needs to be a distinction in your database you created so Excel can tell what to sort or not. If done incorrectly the column sorted won't keep its sister information in adjacent column(s) together when sorted…

Design Flaws – Things to *avoid* when creating a database so Excel can distinguish that you have a database when sorting it or other actions:
1. Different Formatting within a column (all data must be same format)
2. Mixing "text" & "values" in same column (must be one or other)
3. No blank row (take your chances)
4. Border separation (use formatting for borders, not Drawing *toolbar*)
5. Column Label formatting isn't different from rest of data
6. Don't add spaces in cells (use alignment (b)s)

Macros – are quick, easy solutions to cutting down on repeating a task over & over again by recoding it once & then executing it again, & again like lightning with a / of a (b) or using shortcut keys: 1st start recording your steps, Tools>Macro>Record New Macro, type in a **name** for your macro (you can add it as a shortcut key if you type in a letter like q, but if you hold down shift & type q your shortcut for that macro will be Ctrl+Shift+q), /ok; now go through all your steps & don't worry if a mistake is made, but correct it and keep going i.e. Right / a cell> Format Cell, /Pattern *tab* & select a light color, /ok; on the little floating *toolbar* /Stop (b).

Run Macro – To apply all your recorded steps onto a cell or range: /in a cell you want your previously recorded macro color applied too, Tools>Macro>Macros, select your Macro & /Run (b) (or use your shortcut Ctrl+q).

Macro (b) – After you've created your macro you can add that macro to a (b) that you can add to your toolbar: Right /any *toolbar*>Customize, /Commands *tab* & under "Categories" /Macros & from right drag "Custom Button" onto *toolbar*, Right /it & for name type a **name** ® Right /(b)>Assign Macro & select your macro ® & X *pane*.

Delete or Edit Macro – Unless you know Visual Basic programming never try to edit your Macro, but delete it and re-record it: Tools>Macro>Macros, select your Macro & /Delete.

Customize Menus – to create your own menu with menu items like "Save as" & "Copy" (b)s: Tools> Customize, /Commands *tab*, under "Categories" select "New Menu" & in right *pane* / & drag "New Menu" up on your Menu *bar*, to the right of "Help" (b), Under "Categories" scroll & /File & in right *pane* drag "Save as" onto your New Menu. In "Categories" /Edit, in right *pane* drag Copy to Menu. To name your menu: Right /your Menu & change Name to a new **name**, X the *panel* & test your new menu…

Remove – Tools>Customize & drag your New menu off into a blank area, X *panel*

Custom Toolbar – to create your own customer toolbar with toolbar items like "Save as" & "Copy": Tools>Customize, /Toolbars *tab*, /New (b) & name your toolbar, /ok, /Commands

Button (b)	Enter or Return ®	Close X

49

tab, under "Categories" /File & in right *pane* / & drag "Save as" onto your new toolbar. Under "Categories" /Edit, in right *pane* / & drag "Copy" onto toolbar. X *panel* & test.

> Remove – to remove *toolbar*: Tools>Customize, /Toolbars *tab* & either uncheck your toolbar or select it & /Delete (b), X *panel*. To remove Buttons: Tools>Customize, & on any *toolbar* you can / & drag their (b)s off in to a blank area & let go.

> Reset – If you accidentally remove a (b) from the standard or formatting *toolbars* you can bring them all back when you Reset them: Tools>Customize, /Toolbar *tab*, select the toolbar you're missing buttons from either Standard or Formatting & /Reset (b), X *panel*

Conditional Formatting – to apply formatting to cells when criteria is met i.e. a range of cells for sales is less than $10,000: Select the range of cells & Format>Conditional Format, /2nd *arrow*>Less Than & in last *field* type **10000**, /Format (b) & select your formatting i.e. color red, /ok, /ok

Validation – This is a rule that locks a cell(s) to accept only certain #s i.e. say when it came to ordering products like toothpaste the minimum order is 5 & max is 27 tubes:
1. 1st select the cell or range of cells you'd like this rule to apply to,
2. Data>Validation, /Allow *arrow*>Whole # & for minimum type **5**, & maximum type **27**, /Input Message *tab*, /Title *field* & type the name or your error, press Tab *key* & type in your error **message**.

> Remove – Select cell(s) & Data>Validation & /Clear all (b)

> List – To create a cell that contains a list of #'s for a user to choose from: First enter the #'s you want, as a list, in their individual cells somewhere in your spreadsheet i.e. #'s like 1, 2, 3 & 4. Then / in a blank cell you'd like those #'s displayed as a list & Data>Validation, /Allow *arrow*>List & /Source collapse dialogue box (b) (or tiny red *arrow*) and using the mouse select the range of your #'s 1, 2, 3 & 4 & hit ® & /ok. Now /in your blank cell you designated to contain your list & then /it's *arrow*>1, 2, 3 or 4.

Protect Worksheets – To lock cells from others changing them (By default ALL cells are locked, but are only effective when you protect them): Select a range of cells you *want* others to have access to or the ability to change, Right /your selection>Format Cells, /Protection *tab* & remove check from "Locked" & Tools>Protection>Protect Sheet.

> Unprotect: Tools>Protection>Unprotect Sheet.

Protect Workbook – to protect Structure or Worksheets from being edited i.e. to prevent worksheet tabs from being moved: Tools>Protection>Protect Workbook, /ok

Shared Workbook – to use a network folder to save the workbook on so others can work on it at same time: Open your workbook you'd like to share & Tools>Share Workbook & check "Allow changes by more...", /Advanced *tab*, for "Keep change history for" enter a # (for # of days it will keep track of any changes. Also note under "Update changes," that the shared spreadsheet will update after it's been *saved*), /ok, /ok (Note: up on blue title bar in brackets the

Mouse Click /	To >	Task Pane TP

word [shared]). File>Save as & put it on your Network, /Save (Now other coworkers can open your shared workbook & make changes & then when they're finished, /Save & it will automatically update your workbook).

Share & Protect – This not only allows you to share your workbook at the same time with others, but let's you add a password to prevent users from removing your "tracking changes" option: Tools>Protection>Protect and Share Workbook, check "Sharing with track changes" (Note: You can enter your password to protect the tracking from being removed by others)…

Tracking Changes – This not only allows you to share your workbook at the same time with others, but highlights any changes made by "others," (with different colors for different users) in your original workbook; but only after they save and then you save: Tools>Track Changes>Highlight Changes, check "Track changes while…", /ok (Now any changes made will be highlighted, so when you hover your pointer over them it will show the Name of person who changed it, date & time it changed & what was there before it)

Accept Or Reject Changes – In any "Shared" workbook you can accept or reject changes by: Tools>Track Changes>Accept Or Reject Changes, /ok & choose…

Merging Workbooks – merging data from all workbooks into one, but first the workbook has to be "shared," see *Shared Workbook*: Tools>Compare & Merge Workbooks & select one or Ctrl + / many workbooks, /ok (Now everything will be merged, but to track what changes were made remember to: Tools>Track Changes>Accept Or Reject Changes, /ok…)

Formula Auditing Toolbar – Used to trace values to a formula or vice versa: Right /any *toolbar*> Formula Auditing. /in a cell that a formula depends or is based upon & on *toolbar* /*Dependents*. /in a cell containing a formula & on *toolbar* /*Precedent*:

Evaluate Formulas – An easy way to "view" & "change" all parts of your formula that isn't readily accessible: / in a cell that has a formula in it & on Auditing *toolbar* /Evaluate Formula (b), /Evaluate (b) (to view results or effect of first part of formula that has on the overall outcome), /Evaluate (b) again…

Watch Window – used to view a cell while you're in another part of your sheet or workbook: / a cell you want to view while you move around in your workbook & on Auditing *bar* /Show Watch Window (b) & /Add Watch (b) (Now you can scroll to another part of your workbook with the watch window open & you can //the item in the window to go right to it too!)

Outline – arranges data into groups that can be expanded or collapsed, but data has to be sorted before it can be outlined! Also, make sure your data has an easy to follow outline that will be easy for Excel to pattern and form groups: Data>Group & Outline>Auto Outline. To clear, Data>Group & Outline>Clear Outline.

Scenarios – To create your own scenarios and view them; to toggle quickly through the views too:
1. First create a scenario view (i.e. marketing or budget view), and then select all and any ranges that contain values that are a part of your scenarios projections. Tools>Scenarios, /Add, Name *box* type a **name** for your base or original scenario and in Comments *box* type any necessary comments, /ok, /ok & X.

| Button (b) | Enter or Return ® | Close X |

51

2. Next, Tools>Scenarios, /Add, & in Name *box* type the **name** of your new scenario, /ok, then scroll down and find your cells that you'd like to make your new projections & change their #s, /ok, X

    a. <u>View Scenarios</u> – Tools>Customize, /Commands *tab*, under "Categories" select "Tools", & in right *pane* find then / and drag "Scenario drop-down list" to left of "Undo" on *toolbar*, X & select from drop-down list each scenario.

Goal Seek – Like Solver, but it solves problems with only 1 variable & is based on PMT *function* too i.e. to solve a formula based on the value that you want the formula to return: For example, let's say the only variable we want in our PMT *formula* will be the # of payments made in terms of months because we don't care about how many months we'll be paying for our truck because we have to have it! /in cell containing your PMT *formula* & Tools>Goal Seek, in "To Value" enter a monthly payment, press Tab *key*, /By changing cell's collapse (b), /in cell containing your # of payments ®, /ok

Solver – You know the answer you want, but not the inputs; solver can help when you have more than one variable input. Solver is based on PMT *function* found earlier in these notes: Tools>Add Ins & check "Solver Add-in,"/ok. If you wanted to buy a truck with a monthly payment of $555 and a max term of 52 months, solver can help: (solver can't be perfect, but can come close to desired amounts). /in the cell that contains your PMT *formula* result & Tools>Solver, select "Value of"& in its *field* type our desired monthly payment of **555**, now we need to select the variables or cells solver can change, /By Changing Cells \ *collapse* (b) & /in the cell containing your Principle Amount & type **,** & /in a cell containing your # of payments ®, /Add, /in the same cell containing # of payments & type in "Constraint" *field* 52 (as we don't want the term of our loan to be more than 52 months), /ok, /Solve & if we like the results /ok

Pivot Table & Chart – Performs like AutoFilter, sets up your database to filter through it: /in the middle of your database & Data>PivotTable & PivotChart Report, /Next, /Next, /Finish. Next, / & drag your column *headers* onto their appropriate *fields* (This is guess work as to how you want your Pivot Table to operate and filter. If you put a field in the wrong place, / on that field that's in the wrong cell & drag it out of there and let go of the mouse and try again with some other field).

<u>PivotChart</u> – /Chart Wizard (b) to create a PivotChart

<u>Refresh</u> – /on your Data Sheet & change your data, then go back to your Pivot Table & on PivotTable *toolbar*, /Refresh (b)

Workspace – if you need to open more than one workbook at a time you can save them as a workspace: Open up 2 or more workbooks & File>Save Workspace as name it, /Save. X all workbooks & File>open your workspace.xlw *file*

Consolidating – Consolidating data from more than one worksheet or book. In other words, taking values from multiple cells & cramming it into one cell that can be expanded to reveal the values from other cells contributing to the total or

| Mouse Click / | To > | Task Pane <u>TP</u> |

consolidated cell; or left collapsed to simply display its total:

Workbook – Consolidating data from multiple books: 1ˢᵗ all your books must be opened that you want consolidated, then go to your master book's sheet that you want your results displayed in & /in a cell, Data>Consolidate, /Collapse (b) & Window>name of your 1ˢᵗ of many books & select a cell with a # in it & ®, /Add… & repeat steps until all your workbooks are added; then put a check mark in "Create links to.." (By checking this, it will put a + sign after you /ok into your margins so you can /on to view the details of those consolidations), /ok

Link Workbooks – Linking books in a formula is like linking sheets, but you need to have all the books opened you want linked. In other words, you can link a cell to another cell in another workbook by itself or as part of a sum formula: /in a blank cell & type **=sum(**   Window>your other work book you want as a part of your linked sum formula, then /in the cell that you want to add, then press + & again Window>your other work book you want as a part of your linked sum formula, then /in the cell that you want to add… & hit ® when finished.

Edit Links – To change a *link* from one book to another (Note: Make sure this new book has the info in the exact same cells you're linking to from the old book): Open the book that you want linked to another aside from its current link, /Update & Edit>Links & select the old *link* & /Change Source, browse & //on your new book you want linked, /ok.

Text To Columns – To break up phrases or groups of words in a cell into their own cells i.e. Say our 1ˢᵗ column in our database has client names, both their First, Last and some Middle Initial. You can break those full names up to have their own columns i.e. a column for First Name, one for Last Name and the 3ʳᵈ for MI. If only one client has a MI, then you have to plan for 3 columns. WARNING! When you convert your Name column into 2 or more columns, Excel will overwrite your adjacent column(s) (to the right), so be sure to plan ahead and insert extra blank columns to accommodate the # of words you plan to break i.e. Column A has at least some people with their First, Last & MI, say Column B has their Address. Column A already counts as 1 column and hence we need two additional columns to accommodate Last Name and MI: Select Columns B & C, Right /them> Insert (Note: because you selected 2 columns & Right /it, two blank columns were inserted). Select Column's A *header* (so whole column is selected) & Data>Text to Columns, select "Delimited," /Next & select the "Delimiter" that breaks up your text i.e. is it a "Space" that separates your First, Last & MI? Then check ONLY that, /Finish

XML Structuring – XML converts the Excel data so it can be used by other not so friendly applications & vice versa…

XML Maps – Saving an Excel worksheet as an .xml file saves only the contents, but to set rules and structure (or layout. For example, think of Pivot Tables, in that you have to layout the structure of the table by dragging fields to places on you worksheet before importing the actual data) of the worksheet you can add XML Schemas, which would be saved in a 2ⁿᵈ file with a .xsd extension (but .xsd requires programming tags, so best to leave that up to the programmers for now, your job is to only import them): After both files are saved: .xml & .xsd, then the person importing (you, the non programmer or front end) would…

| Button (b) | Enter or Return ® | Close X |

1. Open the .xsd to set the stage for where the "data" will be imported on your spreadsheet: Data>XML>XML Source, TP: /XML Maps (b), /Add & browse to find your .xsd file & //it (Note: if you have more than one schema file, but you're not sure which one contains the fields you want to match the .xml data file, then ADD them all), /ok, TP: (Note: your fields of your .xsd file are displayed). If you added 2 or more .xsd files, TP: /XML maps in this workbook's *arrow*>2nd or 3rd schema map, then after you decided which map to use, from TP: / & drag its *fields*, next to each other on your spreadsheet to organize where you want your data to be placed i.e. drag First Name *field*>A5, Last Name *field*>A6 & so on….

2. After you arranged *fields* on your worksheet it's time to import the data into their respective *fields*: from List *toolbar* /Import XML Data, browse to find .xml file & //it.

Shortcuts

Ctrl+S – *Save*

Ctrl+A – Selects *all* adjacent data, and if there's none then it will default & select the entire worksheet. To select entire worksheet / on the blank cell (b) found between the A Column *header* & the 1 Row *header*.

Ctrl+Z – Undo any action.

Ctrl+Y – Redo any undid action.

Ctrl+X – *Cut*

Ctrl+V – *Paste*

Ctrl+F – *Find*

Ctrl+P – *Print*

Ctrl+/ – Selects cells randomly

Ctrl+Home – Cell A1

Ctrl+End – Goes to end of database, not end of spreadsheet.

F4 – Like Format Painter, *but* it only applies to *most recent* format.

F5 – To go to a cell or your personalized named cell or range.

F7 – To spell check

F11 – To quickly create a Column Chart. After you've selected your data press F11

F12 – Save As

Page Down & Up *keys* – Pages down/up 24 rows at a time.

Alt+Page Down & Up – Pages to Right/Left 9 columns.

Shift+/ – Selects cells in blocks

| Mouse Click / | To > | Task Pane TP |

Outlook

E-mail – In Navigation Pane /Inbox & *toolbar* /New (b)...

    <u>To</u> – Type in email address in this field or /To (b) & select a name here & /To (b) & /ok

    <u>CC</u> – Carbon Copy: /CC to send a copy of your email to others

    <u>Subject</u> – In this field type in the subject of your email message

    <u>Body</u> – Below the subject; type in your message

        <u>Format</u> – Select your text in the 'Body' & *menu* Format>Font & select your style, ok

        <u>Spell Check</u> – /Spell Check (b) or press F7

        <u>Attachment</u> – To send email with attachments i.e. Pictures, Word, Excel etc. On *toolbar* /Paperclip (b) & browse to find your file & once found //it to add it to your email.

            <u>Save Attachment</u> – If someone sends you an email with an attached message: //the attached *icon* to open it and select Save & browse to a folder you'd like it saved in & /Save

    <u>Send</u> – To send email on *toolbar* /Send (b)

        <u>Sent</u> – To view all emails you've ever sent: View>Folder List & /Sent Items *folder*

    <u>Save</u> – If you're in the middle of creating an email, but don't have time to finish typing it /Save (Note: The email will then be saved in the "Drafts" *folder*)

    <u>Printing</u> – to print with out print options: /Print (b) on toolbar, otherwise File>Print or Ctrl+P.

    <u>Create Folder</u> – To create a folder(s) to move your emails from Inbox and organize them in: Right /Inbox *folder*>New & type in a name & hit ® (your new folder will be a subfolder, under your Inbox *folder*).

        <u>Move Messages</u> – Make sure you're Inbox is selected and then / and drag your emails from right window to your new folder.

        <u>Copy Messages</u> – to make copies of messages: Select your email, / and hold Ctrl *key* (note your pointer has a + sign indicating a copy) and drag a copy of that message to another folder

Reply – To reply to an email: Open the email & /Reply (b) & type your message (the color of your reply text is in blue) then /Send (Note: if someone sent you an email with an attachment, the attachment won't be sent back in your reply, but you must use Forward and re-enter their email address in To *field*)

    <u>InfoBar</u> – is a long, light gray box found under the toolbar of emails that displays actions you've done i.e. replied date and time, or other actions that may be needed i.e. follow ups.

    <u>Reply To All</u> – When someone sends you an email and has Carbon Copied it to others you can reply to ALL of them including those CC'd: Open the email & /Reply To All (b) & type your message & /Send

Forward – To pass an email with its original attachments on to someone else: Open email *toolbar* /Forward (b) & in To *field* enter email addresses you'd like the message forwarded to

---

Button (b)	Enter or Return ®	Close X

Inbox – Contains all mail received & to receive email on *toolbar* /Send Receive (b)

    <u>Reading Pane</u> – Splits the Outlook window so user can see icons of emails on left side and a preview of their messages on the right. To turn off Reading Pane: View>Reading Pane> Off

    <u>Sort</u> – To sort emails: By Date /Received *bar* & /it again to sort again either ascending or descending.

    <u>Mark Unread</u> – To mark email as unread after you opened it and want a reminder to read it again: Right email>"mark as unread."

    <u>Deleted Mail</u> – Goes to Recycle Bin folder and sits there until deleted a 2nd time. To delete mail permanently or 2nd time: On Outlook bar /Recycle *folder* & delete the email.

Recall – To recall a sent message; and a message can only be recalled if:

1. It has not been opened.
2. It has not been moved out of Inbox.
3. The receiver is running Outlook and is logged in.

View>Folder List, /Sent Items *folder* & in that *folder* //a sent message & in its *menu* select Actions>Recall This Message… /ok. /Inbox & //the email reply for answer.

Message Settings – used only to tell receiver how to treat the message that will be displayed when received and nothing more i.e.

1. <u>Importance</u> – Low, Normal & High
2. <u>Sensitivity</u> – Normal, Personal, Private & Confidential and is displayed after user opens up email, up top, on the InfoBar.

/New Email (b), /Options (b) & select your "Importance" and/or "Sensitivity" options.

Delivery Options – how, when and where to send your email: /New Email (b), on *toolbar* /Options (b) & when your through following the 4 steps below, /Close (b) & /Send (b) (Note: even though you / send, this email will sit in your "Outbox," until designated time. To send and receive automatically: Tools>Options, /Mail Setup *tab*, /Send Receive (b) & check "Schedule an automatic Send Receive every…" & select your minutes. Be sure to leave computer on & outlook open to send automatically).

1. <u>Forward Replies</u> – Type in an email address in the "Have replies sent to:" *field* (if you want to forward to more than one address, use semicolons ; between each address).
2. <u>Save Copies of Messages</u> – /Browse (b) for 'Save sent message to:' and select a folder you would rather save copies of your sent messages to rather than the default 'Sent Items' *folder*.
3. <u>Delay Mail Delivery</u> – check "Do not deliver before:" & /corresponding *arrows*>date and time. The mail sits in your 'Outbox' until your specified time, and from that point forward you can /Send & Receive (b) and the mail will be sent then, or if your email sends out automatically, again, it will only be sent at the time you specified (Note: to send and receive automatically: Tools>Options, /Mail Setup *tab*, /Send Receive (b) & check 'Schedule an automatic Send Receive every…' & select your minutes. Be sure to leave computer on & outlook open to send automatically).
4. <u>Expire Your Messages</u> – messages that aren't read within a certain time will have a line through them to show it has expired. Great for emails you send

with special, limited time offers. Check "Expires after:" & /corresponding *arrows*>date and time.

Message Formats – format in which an email is composed and or read in i.e. plain text, rich text or HTML:

1. <u>Plain Text</u> – messages won't look distorted to those who receive your email in their program that can't handle formatted messages
2. <u>Rich Text</u> – messages allow you to format text of your email to look nicer
3. <u>HTML</u> – or Hypertext Markup Language messages allow you to send emails with pictures as a background that can contain hyperlinks too.

Tools>Options, /Mail Format *tab*, /Compose in this message format *arrow*>a message format, /ok.

Distribution List – can be programmed to contain one word that when entered in "To:" *field*, will send your email to the group of people you entered into that distribution list: File>New>Distribution List & type a **name** for this group of emails, /Select Members (b), & using Ctrl *key* select a few contacts & /Members (b), /ok (Note: you won't have a list if you haven't created any contacts with email addresses, but you don't have to create a new contact to arbitrarily add an email, simple /Add New (b)), /Save & Close & Close book. /New email (b), /To (b), & select the **name** of your Distribution *list* & /To (b), /ok. & type your email & /Send when done

  <u>Edit Distribution List</u> – Once created the list is added as a contact to your Contacts *folder*: Go to Contacts *folder* & // the **name** of your Distribution *list*.

Assign Task – When you assign a task to someone it gets deleted from your Task *list* & is assigned if accepted, but if not then upon return of declined task you have the option to put it back into your Task *list*. After you /Assign (b), notice: half way down you can check a couple of boxes... One to check is that anytime the person updates task or completes it, you'll get an email that will update the task in your task pad or mark it complete, but that action will only occur after you receive and open their email): /New Task (b), /Assign Task (b), in "To:" *field* type an **email address** & fill out task with due date…, /Send.

  <u>Receiver</u>: In Inbox, open the "Task Request:" & on *toolbar* /Accept (b) (or Decline (b)) & select 'Edit the Response before sending, /ok & type in a **message**, /Send

  <u>Sending Task Updates</u>: to send the person who assigned you the task update(s).

    <u>Receiver</u>: In your Tasks, //The task you accepted, /Status *arrow*>a message of your choice & for %Complete type a #, in message box above original message type in a desired **message**, /Detail *tab* & note the "Update List" has the email address of the person this will update to once you save this task with the changes.

    <u>Sender</u>: When you open a "Declined Task" there's a new (b), "Return Task to List," that you can /on to put the declined task back into your Tasks.

  <u>Assigning Defaults</u>: programming all your assigned tasks to have the same default settings:

    Tools>Options, /Task Options (b) & check or uncheck desired options, /ok

  <u>Sharing</u>: to share a task without assigning it to anyone: Right / a task>Forward, enter **email**, /Send.

Button (b)	Enter or Return ®	Close X

> Receiver: Opens the task sent via email & File>Copy to folder, /Tasks *folder*, /ok

Multiple Message Sorting – Sorting messages with multiple criteria: Underneath any emails you have in your message window, in a blank area, Right / a white, blank area>Sort, /Sort items by *arrow*>any choice, /Then by *arrow*>a second choice, /ok

Finding Messages – *Toolbar* /Find (b), in "Look for:" *field* type a **name**, /Search In *arrow*> All Mail Folders, /Find Now (b)… /Clear to clear findings and go back to normal, or /Find (b) again to remove "Find" *bar*.
> Advance Find – With "Find" *bar* open, /Options *arrow*>Advanced Find… (Note: as long as your Advance Find is open and you receive another message with same criteria, it will show up in your Advance Find as well as your Inbox). Also there are two more advanced find features under the Tools *menu*: Tools>Find>Find Related Messages or Messages From Sender. Type a **name** to find, & to find those with attachments, from here, you can /In *arrow*>subject field and message body, /More choices *tab* & check 'Only items with' one or more attachments & /Find Now (b)
> Filtering Messages – hiding unwanted messages for a time in a specific folder: Right / a blank area of message *window*>Filter & in From *field* type in an **email** address, /ok (Note: below Toolbar, the status reads (Filter Applied).
>> Remove Filter: Right / a blank area of message *window*>Filter, /Clear All (b), /ok

Coloring Messages – applying specific colors to emails sent from certain people: Tools>Organize, /Using Colors *link*, /Apply Color & the color red (default color) will be applied to the email (and ALL emails from same sender, and ONLY in your Inbox) you have selected below in the Inbox's message window.

Rules Wizard – Creating criteria for incoming messages, like email with a specific word(s) to move to a designated folder: Tools>Rules and Alerts (have to be in Inbox to find Rules Wiz), /New Rule (b), select "Start From a Blank Rule," /Next, *check* "with specific words in the subject" & in bottom *pane* /specified words *link* & type a **word**, /Add (to add more words, type them & keep /Add), /ok, /Next & select 'move it to the specified folder' & in bottom *pane* /specified folder *link* & select "a *folder*," /New (b) (to create a new folder as a subfolder to the folder you just selected and to move the emails with certain words to) & type a **name**, /ok, /no, /ok, /Next, & for exceptions select "except if the subject or body contains specific…" & in *pane* below /specific words *link* & type a **word** that is an exception and will keep the email from being move to your new folder, /Add, /ok, /Next & check 'Run this rule now…' /Finish, /ok To see your new folder: In Navigation Pane / + sign left of the folder you selected earlier in the wiz and created your new folder in.

Junk Email – to filter out junk email, to set filter options: Tools>Options, /Preferences *tab*, /Junk E-mail (b). To add future emails from a sender to the Junk Email *folder*: Right /sender's email>

Junk Email>Add Sender to Blocked Sender's List.

Stationary – Applying background colors or themes to your emails: /Inbox, Tools>Options, /Mail Format *tab*, /Compose in this message format *arrow*>HTML, /Stationary Picker (b) & select any stationary & /ok. /New Email (b) (New Mail Message) to see your new background.

> Customize: Tools>Options, /Mail Format *tab*, /Stationary Picker (b), /New (b) & type in a **name**, /Next & select Color & /its *arrow*>any color to be applied as the background to your emails, /ok, /ok, /Fonts (b) & /Choose Font (b) for "When composing a new message," & choose some styles for your text that will stand out from the background color you chose…, /ok & select "Always use my fonts," /ok, /ok. /New Email (b) to see your customized stationary.

Signatures – To send every email with a signature in its body i.e. Your Name with your title *President*: Tools>Options, /Mail Format *tab*, /Signature (b), /New & type in your name, /Next & use Font & create your own… /Finish, /ok, /ok. (/Inbox, /New message & notice your new signature in body of message)

> Block – To keep block signature from being added to every new message: Back in Outlook *menu*: Tools>Options, /Mail Format *tab*, /Signatures for new message *arrow*> None, /ok

> Change – If you created more than one signature you can change your sig in an email: In your new email Right /your signature>your new sig

Categorizing Messages – Assigning messages into categories can make the search through hundreds of emails easier if the user could narrow down the search to related groups: Right /an email> Categories, & check a category, /ok…

> Group By Categories – Right / a blank area in your message window>Group By, /Group items by *arrow*>Categories

> > Ungroup: Right / a blank area>Group By, /Clear All (b)

Votes – To send out emails with voting buttons i.e. Accept or Reject to have pizza at your party instead of doughnuts: In Mail message on *toolbar* /Options (b) & /Use Voting Button's *arrow*> your choice (Note: once choice is added you can edit the default text and add more choices by using semi-colon i.e. Doughnuts; Salad; New Car! And doing this will create buttons in upper left corner of email that can be seen only by recipient). Address & send email & wait, & then you must open up each response or the following won't work…

> Tally Votes – View>Folder List, /Sent Items & open email that was sent to all voters & / its Tracking *tab* & info bar displays the tally of your votes.

Calendar – Schedule appointments…

Appointment – To create a calendar appointment: Navigation Pane /Calendar, *toolbar* /New (b) & fill in the info (Note: check "Reminder" *box* and set time for Outlook to pop-up a reminder, the reminder will only pop-up when Outlook is open. If Outlook isn't open, the pop-up will occur after you open Outlook, so make sure to leave Outlook open to avoid late pop-ups).

| Button (b) | Enter or Return ® | Close X |

Recurring – An appointment that occurs every Monday for example. Open your appointment, & on *toolbar* /Recurrence (b) & select appropriate times.

Active – To see Active Appointments: View>Arrange By>Current View>Active Appointments

Categorize – To assign Appointment a Category: Open your appointment & in lower-right /Categories (b) & check one. To view your appointments by Categories: Close out of your appointment & *menu* View>Arrange By>Current View>By Category (Note: to back to original view: View>Arrange By>Current View>Day/Week/Month)

Event – Is nothing more than an Appointment scheduled all day: Open your appointment & check Event *box* (Note: you can schedule other appointments or more events that same day)

Meeting – Is an appointment that others are invited to Accept or reject, hence a meeting: Open an appointment & on its *toolbar* /Invite Attendees (b), /To (b) to select email (Note: The person you're invited will fall into the 'Required,' or 'Optional' category. The 'Resources' category is to schedule conference rooms, projectors etc.), or type them in using a semi-colon as a separator & /Send when done

Replying – 1st open your "Invite" *mail* & on its *toolbar* /Calendar (b) to immediately view the requested date (The requested date will show what sender has blocked out and if you have something scheduled at the same time then it will show both, crunched in same time. Outlook will allow in this case over scheduling) and see if you have it available, then /Accept or Reject (Note: If you /Accept or Tentative the meeting will automatically be entered into your calendar after you hit Send (b))

Track Replies – To tally the yeahs & the nays: Remember, to track you MUST first open all emails. Go to Calendar & //on meeting you invited others to attend & /Tracking *tab*

Propose Time – Instead of accepting a meeting request; reply with a suggested time: Open Meeting request email & /Propose New Time & select a time & /Send (Now your new proposed meeting is scheduled on your calendar)

Update Meeting – If you have to make a change to the times of your meeting you can send an email update: In Calendar //a Meeting that has already been scheduled & /Scheduling *tab* and find its original time and drag its start & finish lines to different times...& on *toolbar* /Send Update

Cancel Meeting – 1st delete a meeting from your Calendar & select "Send Cancellation & Delete Meeting," /ok & if you'd like type a message & /Send (Note: when recipient opens your message, a prompt to delete meeting from his calendar only if previously accepted)

Default Times – changing calendar's default work days or time: Tools>Options, on Preferences *tab*, /Calendar Options (b), *check* to add or remove days to your calendars "Work Week" *view*, and times too, also you can /Add Holidays to add U.S. holidays to your calendar, /ok, /ok

2 Time Zones – adding an additional time zone to compare & contrast with current one. Only displays in calendars view's 1 day or 5 Work Week: Go to Calendar, on *toolbar* /1 Day (b) & Right /the tan vertical bar that displays the times by hours>Change Time Zone & check "Show additional time zone" & choose your zone & enter a **label** for it, /ok.

Conditional Formatting – To apply specific colors to appointments that contain specific word(s): In the Calendar, on *toolbar*, /Calendar Coloring (b)>Automatic Formatting, /Add & type a **name** for this condition, /Label *arrow*>a color (or category), /Condition (b), & type **word** or phrase, /ok, /ok. **Forwarding Contacts or Notes** – to other people to have a copy of in their Outlook: In your Contacts *folder* Right/ a contact>Forward & enter an email address & /Send.

> Receiver – The receiver of your contact opens their email, //the Contact & /Save & Close to save it to their Contacts (Note: if you receiver already has a copy of a contact, then a message will pop warning them of a duplicate).

> Notes – Forwarding note follow same steps (concept) above...

Contacts – Your very own personal address book: In Outlook *bar* /Contacts & /New (b).
> Category – To put your contacts into viewable categories: Open a contact & in lower-right *corner* /Categories (b) & select one OR /Master Category & type in your new category & /Save & Close
>> Phone List View – A nice simple way of viewing your categorized contacts: View> Current View>Phone List
> Find Contacts – On *toolbar* /in Find Contact *box* & type in a name & hit®
> Map Address – Open up a contact & on toolbar /Display Map of Address (b) that will open up internet and show a map. / on map to zoom in.

Mail Merge by Contact Categories – Creating one formal letter and then creating copies of it and addressing it to a specific category(s) of contacts from your Contacts folder; where the only parts that change on the "copies" are the Names & Addresses, Phone #s, and other fields from your contacts.
Before starting, make sure you have
> ✓ A Letter typed up and...
> ✓ A database i.e. all your contact information entered in Outlook including their names & address or other info that you'll later merge in certain parts on your Letter

After you have created your letter, X it, open Outlook, expand those contacts from one category and using SHIFT or CTRL *key* (to select non-linearly), select all the contacts in that category you want to merge into your recently created letter, Tools> Mail Merge, select "Only selected contacts" then select "Existing document:" & /its Browse (b) to find & //your letter, /ok (Your letter will open up)...
In your letter, / in a place you'd like to place your contact's address, then on Mail Merge *toolbar* /Insert Merge Fields (b), in *window* select "Address Fields" (as it's less confusing figuring out the field's names), & select "Address 1," /Insert (b), /X (b) (You've inserted what is called a "Merge Field,"), now finish inserting the rest of the *fields* in their appropriate places on the letter.
On Mail Merge *toolbar* /View Merged Data (b) & those fields you inserted will convert... to give you an idea what the final letter will look like starting with the 1st record; on the *toolbar*, you can /Next Record *arrow* to advance & view the rest of the

| Button (b) | Enter or Return ® | Close X |

records.

Mail Merge *toolbar* /Merge to New Document (b) (This will allow you to edit or personalize each contact individually) (Note: Every time you open back up your merged document for later editing, /Yes to the question & /ok. Also note that any changes you've made with one of your contacts in Outlook, it won't update in your letter, but instead mail merge again with the steps above – but you won't have to enter the Merge *fields* again)

Link Contacts – to other files in Outlook *folders* (like Inbox for emails) or other files outside of Outlook, so when you open up your contact you can /Activities *tab* and have one-stop-shopping access to those linked items: Open up a contact & from *menu* Action>Link>Items (or Files) and select a *folder*, then select the item(s) in that folder (use Ctrl *key* to select multiple items), /ok. (Note: if no email related message are listed with this contact they may be deleted from your folder, but to be sure /Show *arrow*>All Items and Outlook will do a quick scan of all its folders and display any corresponding emails that match the email address you have listed in the email *field* of your contact)
Use Links: In your contact /Activities *tab*...

Export Contacts To Excel – File>Import & Export, select "Export to a file" /Next, select "Microsoft Excel" /Next, /Contacts *folder*, /Next & /Browse (b) & type a file **name** of the Excel workbook you're exporting to select a place to save it, /Next, /Map Custom Fields (b), /Clear Map (b), from the left *pane* drag any *titles* you want exported over to the right *pane*…, /ok, /Finish.

Tasks – To create a to-do *list*: In Outlook *bar* /Task (b) & in upper-right *corner* /New (b) (Note: REMINDERS will only pop-up as long as you have Outlook opened)
Check off Task – You can check the check box of the task when it's completed and it crosses a line through it to show completed, but you'll have to delete it yourself if you want it removed from your Task list.

Notes – Act like real sticky notes only they're virtual and you can put them almost anywhere on your computer as little reminders: In Outlook *bar* /Notes, /New (b) & type in your note & /it's X to close it & it will show in Notes *folder*... (Note: You can also / & drag Note to your Desktop to store it there too).
Detail View – A different way to view your notes: View>Current View>Notes List
Assign to a Contact – In Notes, Open a Note & /its upper-left *corner* icon>Contacts & assign a contact & close Note. (Open that contact & /Activities *tab* to see Note has been assigned)
Assign to a Category – Open a Note & / its upper-left corner>Categories. To view Notes by their categories: View>Arrange By>Current View>By Category

Journal – manually recording journal entry: Bottom of Navigation Pane / Folder List (b), at top of Pane /Green Journal *icon*, if it asks to automatically record /No (Note: Journal can automatically keep track and record all emails, notes, appointments and assigned tasks and other office applications, but it's better to keep track of these on the Activities in their Contacts file: *see Contacts Link Items*). /New (b) (to manually create a new Journal Entry), enter pertinent info (Note: The timer will record by minutes, and will save and add your time as many times as you toggle between 'Start' and 'Pause' timer). /Save & Close when finished.

| Mouse Click / | To > | Task Pane TP |

Customize Toolbar – Adding or removing (b)s from your toolbars: /Inbox & at very end of *toolbar*, /Toolbar Options *arrow*>Add or Remove Buttons>Standard & check to add a (b) or uncheck to remove one, or Right /Toolbar>Customize, /Commands *tab* & under "Categories" select 'Edit' & under 'Commands' you can / & drag 'Cut' or 'Copy' next to the rest of the (b)s on the *toolbar* above (Note: you can't drag new (b)s anywhere, they have to be next to the current (b)s on your toolbar).

Remove: Right /Toolbar>Customize & with the Customize box open you can / & drag (b) off the toolbar into a blank area and the (b) will disappear.

New Toolbar – Right */Toolbar*>Customize, /Toolbars *tab*, /New & type a **name**, /ok, /Commands *tab* & add any (b)s from under the 'Commands' *pane* by / & drag to your new *toolbar*.

Delete Toolbar: Right */Toolbar*>Customize, /Toolbar *tab*, select your toolbar & /Delete (b).

New Menu – Right */toolbar*>Customize, /Commands *tab*, under 'Categories' select 'New Menu,' & under 'Commands' / & drag 'New Menu' above *toolbar* & next to the Help *menu* & Right /it & in Name type a **name**. Then drag a few commands like Copy or Paste to it… To delete the menu, / & drag it off to a blank area (Note: the Customize box has to be open to remove menus or make any changes to the toolbars).

Outlook Homepage – To set Outlooks *folder* in Navigation Pane to have a web homepage: In Navigation Page Right /Outlook *icon*>Properties, /Home Page *tab*, in "Address" *field* type **a website address**, (Note: To restore default /Restore Default (b)), /ok…

MSN Messenger – Instant messaging over the internet

Hotmail – Before you can use MSN Messenger you have to have a Hotmail or .NET Passport account (When you sign up for Hotmail it also acts as a .NET Passport account): Go to the website **www.msn.com** & /Hot Mail *link*, /New Account Sign Up *link* and follow direction to obtain your Hotmail account.

Add Hotmail Address To Outlook – If you want, you can add your hotmail address to Outlook: Open Outlook, Tools>Email Accounts /Next, /Add (b), select HTTP /Next, type in **your name**, **email address**, & /HTTP Mail Service Provider *arrow*>Hotmail, and type in your password /Next, /Finish.

Windows Messenger – If you're using Windows XP Operating System: /Start>All Programs>Online Services (Or Windows Messenger)> Windows Messenger and it ought to automatically pull up Windows Messenger and sign you in.

Add Contacts – Adding other people to instant message to in your contacts book: Bottom of your Windows Messenger *window* /+Add a Contact *link*, select "By e-mail address or sign-in name" /Next, type in **email address** /Next, /Finish.

Remove Contact – Tools>Manage Contacts>Delete Contact…

Send An Instant Message – /Send an Instant Message *link*, & select a person you want to instant message, /ok, a

| Button (b) | Enter or Return ® | Close X |

new *window* will open up and you can start typing in your message & hit ® or /Send (b) (Note: you can close your smaller slimmer window and it will minimize to bottom-right of your Task Bar, called the System Tray, and when you want to bring it back Right /the green person *icon*>Open) Note: you can minimize your conversation *window* also to the Taskbar and when you get IM (Instant Message) it will flash red and a little window will pop up

File Attachments – to attach a file to your instant message: in Conversation *window* /Send a File or Photo *link* and browse to find one and //it to send.

Status – is to let your contacts know if you're busy: If your Windows Messenger is opened, up at top /the *arrow* next to your name>a choice i.e. busy, out to lunch etc. or, you can Right / the green person *icon* below in the System Tray>My Status> busy and your contacts won't be able to send you and IM.

Preferences – to set you IM options: In Windows Messenger *window* Tools>Options, /Preferences *tab*, here you can increase or decrease the minutes to display the Status "Away" if your haven't been using IM lately (Note: if you don't use your IM, you lose contact until you change your status from "Away" to "Online")

Search Folders – are folders that contain shortcuts of items that match a certain criteria you set, and because they're copies, deleting a Search Folder won't delete these items, BUT you can open up that item from the Search Folder and delete it. It's a way to organize items into one folder without having to search in several folders.

Create Search Folder – /Inbox, File>New>Search Folder, select "Mail From Specific People," /Choose & select a name, /ok, /ok (Note: it will search all Outlook *folders* except the "Deleted Items" *folder*).

Archiving – moves what you choose from Outlook's messages, tasks, contacts and notes in another location that you can import later if so desired: File>Archive & select Inbox, /Archive items older than *arrow*>Today's Date, /ok.

To Import Back: File>Import and Export & select "Import from another program or file," /Next & select "Personal Folder File (.pst)" /Next, /Browse (b) & //Archive.pst, /Next & select Inbox, /Finish (Note: import will copy from the archive folder you data, so you'll still have your originals in the archive). View>Folder List & delete Inbox.

Automatic Archiving: Right /Inbox>Properties, /AutoArchive *tab*

Protect Archive – You can put a password to your Archive *folder* so nobody can access it: File>Data File Management, select "Archive Folder," /Settings (b), /Change Password (b) and enter password.

Microsoft Exchange Server – The following office actions will only be found and work in Outlook if your company has a Microsoft Exchange Server.

Out Of Office – the office assistant sends an "out of office" message. (Note: the Out of Office Assistant will only show up in your Tools *menu* if your office has you set up on a Microsoft

Exchange Server). Tools>Out of Office Asst., select "I am currently Out of the Office" and type in the "AutoReply Only Once To Each Sender With The Following Text" *field* **I'm out of office and back soon**, /Add Rule…

Exceptions – you can let specified emails be forwarded to your coworker: In the Edit Rule *window*, /From (b), /Show Names *arrow*>a contact and select him or her, /ok. Under "Perform These Actions" *check* "Forward" and next to it /To (b), /Show Names *arrow* and // any contact to add, /ok, /ok

Turn Off – Tools>Out Of Office Assistant & select "I am currently In the Office," /ok

Share Folders – (Note: Sharing folders will only be available if your office has you set up on a Microsoft Exchange Server).

Setting Folder Permissions – to specify what type, if any, access ALL users have to your shared folder, i.e. modify, read-only, deleting or adding (Note: this will give ALL users access to your folder, but again you can limit what ALL these users can do; to limit access to certain users *see Delegating Access*): In Navigation Pane /Contacts, and above that /Share My Contacts *link*, /Permission Level *arrow*>one of the following settings:

    a. None – You can't open folder

    b. Owner – gives anyone access to do anything including changing the folders permission levels on you!

    c. Publishing Editor – has complete access except can't modify folder's permission

    d. Editor – Can't create subfolders or change folder's permission levels

    e. Publishing Author – Can't change folder's permission levels, can only modify and or delete their own works they've added to the folder

    f. Author – same as Publishing Author except can't create subfolders

    g. Reviewer – Can only read

    h. Contributor – Can't read, modify, delete, but only create

/ok (Note: You can exclude certain contacts from being read from a user with permission to see all: Open a contact you want to make private from others you are sharing, and at the bottom right of your contact *check* "Private," /Save & Close (b))

Delegating Access – to specify what type access a specified user(s) have to your shared folder: At bottom of Navigation Pane /Folder List, then at top /Calendar *icon*, then Right /it>Properties, /Permissions *tab*, /Add, //a persons name, /ok & select below options of permissions, /ok

Accessing A User's Shared Folder – File>Open>Other User's Folder, /Name (b), //somebody's name, /ok (Note: If you opened a shared calendar, both yours and the sharer's will be viewed side-by-side in your window). To hide the sharer's calendar: In Navigation Pane uncheck his or her name

Button (b)	Enter or Return ®	Close X

PowerPoint

Wizard – to quickly create a several slide Presentation, based upon your selection from the preformatted templates: File>New, <u>TP</u>: /From AutoContent wizard, /Next & /a Category (b), /Next & follow the rest of the wizard's prompts…, /Finish.

Templates – Individual slides that are preformatted for you: Right /blank area of your slide>Slide Design, <u>TP</u>: scroll down & Right /your choice>Apply to all or one of your slides…

Background – to apply a color(s) or pictures to one slide or all: Right /a blank part of the slide> Background, /*arrow*>Fill Effects & /Gradients *tab* to chose either a single color or a collage of them called Gradients, or /Picture *tab*, /Select Picture (b) & browse to find your picture, //it, /ok, /Apply to All or Apply…

Add Slides – To add more slides to your presentation: Right /a blank part of a slide>Slide Layout, <u>TP</u> find a desired slide & Right /it>Insert New Slide.

Change Slide – To changes a slide's layout: Right /a blank part of your slide>Slide Layout, <u>TP</u>: find & Right /a desired slide>Apply to Selected Slides.

Formatting Text – To change the formatting of your text: Select your text & Format>Font (or Ctrl+T)
    <u>Line or Bullet Spacing</u> – To create single or double spaced bullets or lines in your text: 1st select your text or bullets & Format>Line Spacing & increase spacing>your choice, /ok
    <u>Indents</u> – To indent your text or bullets all at once: 1st make sure your horizontal ruler is showing by View>Ruler, then select your bullets or text. On H-ruler grab the "Left Indent" *marker* (Looks like a little box under attached little triangle) & drag right an inch (Note: Left Marker has 3 choices: Top, inverted *triangle* moves the bullet when / & dragged, Middle *triangle* moves the text only when dragged, & bottom *square* moves both text & bullet when dragged by mouse)

Slide View – By default when you open PowerPoint the left side of your screen has an Edit *bar* with 2 *tabs* (One Slide & other Outline), and Slide is selected. (Note: you can X this bar, but if you want it back in View>Normal (Restore Panes))

Outline View – This view is to edit the text of your slides in an easier to manage "Outline View": On left side of screen /Outline *tab*

Table – Creates many cells to place and organize text in: Insert>Table & type in your **rows** & **columns**, /ok. All you need to add or remove rows, columns and cells, is on the Tables & Borders *toolbar* using its Table (b) *arrow* or Right /a cell in your table> delete or insert.
    <u>Borders & Fill</u> – To add color to your table's borders or shading to cells: 1st select your table (a row, column or cell) you want to apply color & Right /your selection (or the *fuzzy*

border of your table to format whole table)>Borders & Fill (Note: if you are trying to apply a border style or color to a border around your table or cell, be sure that after you select your style (or color) be sure to /in diagram on the borders you want them applied to, before you X Borders & Fill)

Cell Dividers – Can be / & drag left or right to give columns or rows of cells more or less spacing.

Chart – Inserting a Slide Chart: Right /a blank spot on any slide>Slide Layout, TP: scroll to its bottom & hover over the Chart *template* & Right /it>Insert Slide. On your new slide //where its says "Double click to add chart" (Brings up a default Chart template that you can delete & add your own data in its floating Datasheet)

Datasheet – When you're done entering your data in the Datasheet don't /the X or its Close *window* (b) (Because if you do, you can't //the chart later to easily open the Datasheet to make data changes to your chart). Instead /in a blank area off of your slide to close your Datasheet & your Chart's edit mode. If you did /the X, the only other way to bring up your Datasheet is a little *tricky* to initially to reset it to open on a //: First //your chart, then Right /the white space between the chart & it's outer *fuzzy* border>Datasheet (Now that you reset it, after you X out of your Datasheet properly, you can go back to //Chart again to open its Datasheet)

Chart Type – To change your chart to a pie, column, or doughnut chart, etc. Make sure your chart is in edit mode (Datasheet is showing, & remember you can //on your chart to open Datasheet) & Chart>Chart Type & select any chart, /ok

Chart Options – To add a Title to your chart, Data Labels etc.: Chart>Chart Options

Insert Picture – Insert>Picture>From File, browse & find your picture, then //it

Drawing Toolbar – Used to make shapes. Remember if you every need a toolbar i.e. Drawing, Right /any available *toolbar*>Drawing (Drawing *toolbar* will appear at the bottom of your PowerPoint Program: To create an object like a circle, on Drawing *toolbar* /on Oval (b), & hold Shift *key* & / & drag on your slide to create a perfect circle. For square /Rectangle & use Shift *key* too.

Selecting Objects – To select several object / on 1st one & hold Shift *key* & / on the others…

Group Objects – To group objects as one: Select 2 or more objects & on *toolbar* /Draw>Group. To ungroup: /Draw>Ungroup.

Align Objects – To align objects perfectly within each other: move an object(s) within a larger one, then select all of your objects, On *toolbar* /Draw>Align or Distribute>Align Center, then go back & /Draw>Align or Distribute>Align Middle. To align 2 or more object's top, bottom or middle together: Select Both Object & *toolbar* /Draw>Align or Distribute>Align Top, Middle or Bottom (Note: if you selected Top, the object that's closest to the Top, say out of 7 you want aligned, will be the control from which the rest of the 6 objects will align their tops to)

Layering – If some objects are hiding behind others and you want them in front: Right /the object you want in front>Order>Bring to Front (Note: Send Backward or Forward brings the object forward one layer at a time, where as Bring to Front brings it completely to first or front layer).

| Button (b) | Enter or Return ® | Close X |

Rotate – Most objects when selected have a green handle (circle) that when / & dragged will rotate your object left or right.

Format – To add color to a shape or object: Select shape & on Drawing *toolbar* /Fill Color (or Paint Bucket) *arrow*>a color or>"Fill Effects" & choose between the 4 *tabs*: Gradient (2 colors or more), Texture (Marble, oak, cork...), Pattern (dots & lines) and Picture (You can insert a picture into your shape by /Select Picture (b) & browsing & //on a picture you want to insert).

AutoShapes – Adding shapes to your presentation with text in them: i.e. On Drawing *toolbar* /AutoShapes (b)>Stars & Banners (or Callouts for cartoon bubbles), & select a Star & use Shift *key* to / & drag a proportional star on your slide & type in some **text** (see Word Wrap!).

Word Wrap – When you type a lot of text it exceeds beyond the border of the shape, have it wrap inside the shape instead: Right /your shape>Format AutoShape, /Text Box *tab* & check Word Wrap, /ok

Change AutoShapes – To change your shape: Select the shape & on *toolbar* /Draw>Change AutoShape>Whatever you want

Format – To add color to a shape or object: Select shape & on Drawing *toolbar* /Fill Color (or Paint Bucket) *arrow*>a color or>"Fill Effects" & choose between the 4 *tabs*: Gradient (2 colors or more), Texture (Marble, oak, cork...), Pattern (dots & lines) & Picture (You can insert a picture into your shape by /Select Picture (b) & browsing & //on a picture you want to insert).

WordArt – Basically it's text with attitude or flair that you can add 3-D effects to: Select your text you want converted to WordArt & on *toolbar* /WordArt (b), //a choice, /ok. To resize your WordArt: / & drag one of its white handles around the WordArt, out or in. To add 3-D effects: /the last button on Drawing *toolbar*>3-D Settings & use that *toolbar* to add effects like lighting, depth & rotations.

Edit – To edit WordArt, select your Art & on WordArt *toolbar*, /Edit Text (b). To change your Art: on WordArt *toolbar*, /WordArt Shape (b) (abc) and select anyshape, /ok

Clip Art – To insert Clip Art on a slide, 1 of 3 ways:
1. Slide Layout – A preformatted slide that has a designated area to insert you ClipArt: Format>Slide Layout, TP: & hover over each slide till you read one that says "Clip Art" & insert it. On that slide //Add Clip Art (b) & select your art & //it.
2. Insert *Menu* – Or insert a blank slide & Insert>Picture> Clipart & TP: in "Search for" *box* type **Cartoons**, /Go (b) & /one.
3. Drawing *Toolbar* – (Right /any available *toolbar*>Drawing) /Insert Clip Art (b), TP: in "Search for" *box* type **Cartoons**, /Go (b) & /one.

Spell Check – To check your presentations spelling: Right /any misspelled word (underlined in red), or to check the whole presentation on *toolbar* /Spell Check (b)

Slide Sorter – A view to: see ALL of your slides, arrange them, & add & see a preview of your slide transitions: View>Slide Sorter

Hide Slide – To hide a slide from displaying in your presentation without deleting it: Right /any

Mouse Click /	To >	Task Pane TP

slide>Hide Slide (Note: your slide # has a gray box around it with a line through it to show it's hidden). To unhide: Right /slide>Hide Slide (to deselect it).

Change Slide Order – If you'd like to rearrange your slides so let's say slide #3 becomes your first slide: /on Slide #3 & drag it before Slide 1

Transitions – In your presentation when you / from one slide to advance to the next; how that slide pops-up, scrolls in etc. on the screen is called a transition: Right /a slide>Slide Transition, TP: select a transition; you can also select its speed, a sound (Note: /Sound *arrow*>Other Sound & browse to find & //your own sound) & whether to activate your slide on Mouse / or after so many seconds.

Speaker Notes – Notes that can be added to each slide & printed out for the presenter to read during their presentation: View>Notes Page & under a slide type a few **notes**. To print slides with accompanying Note Pages: Cntrl+P, /Print What *arrow*>Notes Page

Print Handouts – To print slides for handouts in Black & White (speaker notes or Note Pages aren't included): Cntrl+P, /Print What *arrow*>Handouts.

Presentation To Word – File>Send To>Microsoft Office Word, select any, /ok...

Pack & Go – Pack & Go will not only save your fonts, but with PowerPoint Viewer you can play your presentation on computers that don't even have PowerPoint installed: File>Package for CD, /Copy to Folder (b) & type a **name**, /Browse (b) & select a destination to save it i.e. Desktop, /ok.

Color Scheme – a specified group of colors applied to the presentation i.e. text & background colors: Format>Slide Design, TP: /Color Schemes, & at bottom of TP: /Edit Color Schemes, //Background *square* to change background color etc, /Apply…

Slide Master – If you want the same format, style or image on every slide, all you need to do is change the Slide Master: View>Master>Slide Master, now make your changes i.e. applying a different color to the default text displayed in Master or inserting a picture, & when finished either /Close Master View or continue with *Custom Bullets* below… (Note: By default Slide Master's View doesn't contain a Title Slide Master, & typically the only reason some add Title Masters is because they usually like the formatting of their Title Slides different from the rest of the others: On Slide Master View *toolbar* /Insert New Title Master. Slide Masters are always above and connected by a gray line to their Title Masters below (if any). 2nd Note: You can also create several Master Slide designs & apply them to certain slides throughout your presentation)

Custom Bullets – You can change the default bullets to another symbol, so when you insert a bulleted slide layout in "Normal View" it will use your default symbols. Note: Your custom bullets won't apply from your Master Slide to bullets in a Text Box you created – have to use PowerPoint's default, preformatted bulleted Slide Layouts: In Slide Master, Right /the first bullet>Bullets & Numbering, /Custom (b) & select one… Right /2nd bullet>Bullets & Numbering, /Picture (b) & select one (or here you can /Import (b) & insert your own picture as a bullet), /ok, /Close Master View or continue with *Headers & Footers*…

Button (b)	Enter or Return ®	Close X

Headers & Footers – To add footer to all of your slides like dates, slide numbering & notes: View> Header & Footer (Note: you can apply changes to All Slides or just one you're currently working on. 2nd Note: in "Slide Master" at the bottom you see 3 text boxes & each can be formatted i.e. select the "Number Area" text *box*, Format>Font & select a different color i.e. white, so it can stand out against a black or dark colored slide)

Edit Notes Master – To add more text space by shrinking the slide & stretching the Text Box: View> Master>Notes Master & if you want delete all headers & footers Text *boxes* (4 of them) to free up more room, 4 of them. Drag the slide *picture* to upper-left corner & /it lower-right sizing handle & drag inward to shrink it (Note: on *toolbar* /Zoom *arrow*> 66% to get a closer view), & then drag one of the top handles of the Note's Text *box* up, to stretch it out & when finished, /Close Master View.

Design Template – If you'd like to preserve your current presentation's style to base all of your future presentations off of, then save it as a Template: File>Save as, /File Type *arrow*>Design Template, & type a **name** for your Template, /Save…

    New Presentation – Based on your saved template: 1st close out of your template you just saved, File>Close & then File>New, <u>TP</u>: /On my computer, /General *tab* & //Your Presentation you just saved as a template (Note: You now have a new presentation based off of your template you saved earlier, AND if you now save this new presentation is won't overwrite your template, but save it as another presentation)

Org Chart – To insert an Organization Chart in your slide: On Drawing *toolbar*, /Insert Diagram (b) & //Organization Chart. /on the boxes & type in the **names** of you of your coworkers & their titles.

    Add Boxes – Select an employee box you'd like to add a subordinate, coworker or assistant to, & on Organization Chart *toolbar* /Insert Shape *arrow*>any of the 3.

    Delete Boxes – /on a box & press Delete

    Move Boxes – Hover your pointer over border of a box you want moved till you see 4-way arrow, / & drag it over the box of another employee to change the structure.

    Style – To change the style of your Org Chart: On Chart *toolbar* /AutoFormat (b), select one & /ok.

Diagram – creating graphical designs without the top down design of an Organization chart: Drawing *toolbar* /Insert Diagram (b) & //Venn Diagram (3 overlapping circles), & Right /a circle> delete or insert more circles or to format them. Next to each circle is a small Text *box* (you may have to zoom>100% on *toolbar* to see it), you can use to label your circles. Shift Circles around: select a circle & on Diagram *toolbar* /Move Shape Back (b), or /Change to (b) for more *styles*, or /AutoFormat (b) (to apply custom formatting) & select one, /ok…

Flowchart – a way to display a process with shapes. Meaning of shapes:
1. Capsule – initiates the begging or declares the end of the chart's process
2. Rectangle – a step in the process

| Mouse Click / | To > | Task Pane <u>TP</u> |

3. <u>Diamond</u> – a yes or no decision that splits the process

4. <u>Parallelogram</u> – acquire data step

<u>Grid</u> – is checkerboard horizontal & vertical lines to help you line up shapes.

<u>Guides</u> – a vertical & horizontal line you can / & drag to help line as well.

To turn on grids & guides to help line up your objects: View>Grids & Guides, check "Display grid…" & "Display drawing guides…" /Spacing *arrow*>any (grid spacing), /ok

To break off a *toolbar* from AutoShapes so it can temporarily display before us for easy shape access:

> Drawing *toolbar*, /AutoShapes>Flowchart & move pointer to top of box displaying the shapes, / & grab its *bar* and drag it off…, Repeat, & get "Connectors" dragged off from AutoShapes too (Note: They become floating *toolbars* for easier access, & will always remain in AutoShapes *menu* even after you break them of from *menu*).

> <u>Sample Flow Chart</u> – to create a "Start" & "End" with one Process *box* in the middle named "Eat Doughnut": Flowchart *toolbar*, /Process Shape (1st shape) & / & drag on slide to stretch shape open into a rectangle (say 1x3-inches) & type **Eat Doughnut**, then / & drag a small "Terminator" shape (capsule looking) & Ctrl+D (Creates duplicate), drag all shapes to line up along x-axis with a terminator shape on either side of the process. Select 1st Terminator & type **START** & name 2nd **END**. On Connectors *toolbar* find & /Elbow Arrow Connector, hover over right border of "Start" Terminator, & /on its blue *handle*, then hover over left-side of "Eat Doughnut" Process, /on its blue *handle* to secure it. Connectors *toolbar*, /Elbow Arrow Connector & connect right handle of Process to left blue handle of "End" Terminator (Note: you can / & drag your shapes around, & because of the elbow connector the connectors/lines will bend if you move your Terminators out of a direct line with the Process. 2nd Note: remember when through to hide your lines or they'll always show up when you're designing: View>Grid & Gridlines & uncheck them), /ok.

Movies & Sound – You can attach a sound to an object on its entrance on any slide. (Note: this exercise will only work if you've already created an object & have assigned it an animated effect, *see Animate*). Let's say I've created a circle to fly in & I want the sound of breaking glass upon its mouse clicked entrance: You DON'T need to select the circle, Insert>Movies & Sound>Sound From File & browse through your computer to find your sound, //it & /When clicked (so it doesn't play automatically)…

> <u>Hide Sound</u> – After your sound is inserted you'll see a little speaker representative of your sound. This speaker will also show in your presentation too, but if you only want to hear it & not see it: Right /Sound *icon*>Edit Sound Object & check "Hide…"

> <u>Cue Sound</u> – Select speaker *icon* & Slide Show>Custom Animation TP: Find the "Media" (it will have a Tan "Trigger" title *bar* above it), //it (not the Tab *bar* – brings up properties), /Timing *tab*, /Triggers (b) (to expand to see menu below it) & select "Animate as part of the click sequence" (this allows you control when YOU want to trigger your sound & Tan *bar* will disappear because of selection), then /Start *arrow*> With Previous (so when your object that is already animated comes flying in the sound will start at same time, OR >Start After Previous & below in "Delay" *box* enter as many seconds you want this sound delayed after object fly's in!), /ok & TP: /Play to test!

Button (b)	Enter or Return ®	Close X

Use <u>Default Sounds</u> – if you want to use free sounds from Microsoft: For Example – Drawing *toolbar* /ClipArt (b) <u>TP</u>: under "Search" type **Cheer** & /Result Should be *arrow* & uncheck all except "Sounds," /Go (b). <u>TP</u>: /on Sound to insert it & select "Automatically" or "When Clicked," on when you want that sound played.

<u>Insert Movies</u> – Insert>Movies & Sound>Movie From File, browse & when you find your movie //it (Note: after you //it you could select play "Automatically," but if you select "When Clicked" then during your presentation when you get to that movie slide you'll see a picture of your movie that you can / on to play & / again to pause it. /off your movie picture twice to advanced to next slide. 2nd Note: Your movie might not play if after you inserted the movie from a folder and then you move that folder or delete it, also make sure that folder containing the movie you inserted into your Presentation is on your Desktop, because if you have it buried under several folders, then PowerPoint will have a fit & won't be able to go that deep in the link to find & play your movie during your presentation).

Animate – You can have Bullets, Item List, and any objects to come in on cue with a mouse / on any slide in your presentation: Select your object or text & Slide Show>Custom Animation, <u>TP</u>: /Add Effect>Entrance>any effect.

<u>Order of Effects</u> – If you have more than one object animated in a slide you can have them animate in a order you choose: Select your 1st object (or animated bullet), <u>TP</u>: / & drag the object's animation *bar* in the order you'd like it to animate (Top of the animation list will be 1st)

<u>Effect Timing</u> – once you've established the "Order of Effects" you can pick up the tempo or timing for each animation or delay it: In Custom Animation <u>TP</u>: //an animation *bar* (to bring up it's properties), /Timing *tab*, /Start *arrow*>With Previous or After Previous & in "Delay" *box* enter a time to delay your animation if desired (Note: if you want your first object to start it's animation as soon as you advance to its slide then set it's timing to "With Previous" or "After Previous").

<u>Motion Path</u> – you can create a path for an object to follow during its animation: Select your object, Slide Show>Custom Animation, <u>TP</u>: /Add Effect>Motion Paths>a path of your choice (Note: it will play out your path & when finished it will reveal a line), /Red *arrow* & / & drag its handle (small white circle) diagonally up & left a little (to change path). To add multiple paths to one object: /off in a blank area, select same object, In Custom Animation <u>TP</u>: /Add Effects>Motion Paths>a 2nd path of your choice (Note: it will play out your path & when finished it will reveal the 2nd line), Now drag that 2nd line so the Green *arrow* is over the Red *arrow* of the 1st Motion path (this will continue the path!), /Play (b) to test!

Web Presentation Wiz – Creating a preformatted for Web presentation using AutoContent Wizard that includes links: File>New, <u>TP</u>: /From AutoContent Wizard *link*, /Next, /Corporate & select "Group Home Page," /Next & select "Web Presentation," /Next & follow the rest of the Wizard. When finished Press F5 to start Slide Show (Note: On the left side of your presentation there are several titles that are actual links to other slides in your presentation. Also, note that you can change the design, formatting, text of this presentation to your design).To end show Press Esc *key*

| Mouse Click / | To > | Task Pane <u>TP</u> |

Create Links – Use "Action Settings" to turn your text, pictures or other objects into a link, that when user click's on takes them to another slide, program or website. If you don't want to use your own objects for links then use PowerPoint's "Action Buttons…"

    Action Settings – to link an object or text with specific actions i.e. go to another slide or run a program, play a sound or movie: On slide, type some **text** (or insert an object or picture), that during your presentation when you / on it, you'd like to take you to another slide (or open & run a program i.e. play a movie in Windows Media player. Note: the Windows Media player will open up and play your movie & when it's done, X the movie and you'll be back in your presentation on same slide, before you played your movie). Select the text (or your object), Slide Show>Action Settings (or Right /it>Action Settings), /Hyperlink to, then /its *arrow*>Slide & select a slide (or /its *arrow*>URL & type another website address i.e. **www.disney.com**, or /its *arrow*>Other File & browse to find your movie & //it), /ok, /ok. Press Shift+F5 (runs Slide Show from current slide) & test your *link!*

    Action Buttons – are PowerPoint (b)'s you can use to link internally to other slides, or externally, run programs and play sounds: Slide Show>Action Buttons>an action (b) of your choice & / & drag on your slide to draw the size of your (b), /Hyperlink to *arrow*>any preferences you want that action (b) to perform… i.e. you could have it play a movie (for more details on playing movies, *see Action Settings*) if you /Hyperlink to *arrow*>Other file, browse to find & //your movie file, /ok (Note: to edit Right /(b)>Action Settings, also you don't have to use Action (b)'s you can Right /ClipArt & apply Action Setting to it too). Press Shift+F5 (run slideshow from current slide) to test it!

    Excel Chart – You can insert an Excel Chart you've created, into a slide & have it linked so any changes you make in Excel will update that change in your slide. Your Excel Chart has to have its own Worksheet and can't be embedded as an object next to your data on the same Worksheet, if it is, select your chart & Chart>Location & select "As new sheet," /ok. Your first Worksheet now out to be your chart, /Save & X Excel: In a blank slide Insert> Object, /Create From File, /Browse>a place you have stored your Excel Workbook that contains your chart & //it, check Link *box*, /ok (Note: if you see data & not a chart then //the data on your slide to open up Excel, find your Chart Worksheet & select the Chart on that Worksheet, /Save & X Excel, then in PowerPoint, Right /your Excel's Data>Update Link. This will change your data to your Chart, because what you touched last in Excel & saved, that is what your slide will display!).

        Edit – If you //on your inserted Chart on your slide, this will open up your linked Excel Workbook, or you can open up Excel by itself & make your changes without your Presentation opened. (But remember when you're finished making data changes in Excel, the last thing you do before you save is select your chart & /Save & then X Excel. This is because PowerPoint will link the last thing you touched in Excel; & show that after you update your link to it in your presentation).

            Updating – Either Right /the Chart>Update Link in your slide, or /Save & X PowerPoint & when you reopen it, /Update Links (b)

Publish to Web – To prepare your presentation for the Web: File>Web Page Preview (to test links). File>Save as Web Page, /Publish, /Change & type a **name** that you want others to see up in the blue Title bar when they visit your website (Note: Sometimes it's best to

Button (b)	Enter or Return ®	Close X

publish web pages if a majority of your clients use older versions of web browsers, and under "Browser support" you may want to select "All browsers listed above"), /ok, /Publish (Note: Your web page will be stored in the same *folder* your Presentation was saved in as a .mht file).

Customizing Show – capturing certain slides from your original presentation to create a temporary presentation for a particular audience that doesn't need to see certain parts of your slides. You can create several custom presentations within your original presentation to view for certain audiences: Slide Show>Custom Shows, /New, & for "Slide show name" type a name i.e. **Edited Version**, then find a slide you want to add to it & //it i.e. //Slide 2 (Note: //as many slides to add to this custom presentation) & when finished, /ok, /Show (this runs that custom presentation). Be sure to /Save as all the Custom presentation you add inside your original presentation & then you can use them later, over & over again by opening your original presentation & Slide Show>Custom Shows, select your show, /Show.

Record Narration – To record your voice for each slide. Be sure you have a microphone hooked up to your computer: /Slide 1, Slide Show>Record Narration (Note: your voice will record & embed in presentation unless you check "Link narrations in," in which case you pick a *folder* to embed your recordings into, that's linked to your presentation), /Change Quality (b) /Attributes *arrow* (Note: the higher KHz you go the better the quality but the larger the file), /ok, /Set Microphone Level (b) & speak into your microphone to test if sound meter is picking you up & sets the optimal voice range depending on the loudness or softness of your voice, /ok… /ok & read aloud the slide & when finished / & read next slide & / to advance to next slide & read and so on, but when finished /Save, to record your timings (the amount of time you spent talking on each slide, so when another person views your show, it will play your voice & automatically advance to next slide – based upon the time you spent on each slide during your recording of your narration).

Edit Timing – to edit time spent on each slide before automatically advancing to the next: View> Slide Sorter, Right /a slide>Slide Transition & in TP: edit "Automatically after" setting… then / off in a blank area to see it apply to slide.

Override Timings – to have your presentation ignore your rehearsed timings without erasing them; because maybe you want to advance your slides manually for a presentation (Note: this will also work on for "Automatic Slideshow"): Slide Show>Set Up Show, under "Advance Slides" select "manual," /ok

Timed Slideshow – To assign time to each slide that will automatically advance after its time expires: Go to Slide 1 & Slide Show>Rehearse Timings & watch the timer that pops up & / when you think enough time has been spent on that slide to stop the timer & advance to the next slide & the timer will start up again. Continue till you get to end of your show & /yes to save your timings for each slide.

Repeating Show – You could use your presentation in a kiosk & your Slide Show will go on a continuous loop until somebody hits ESC Key. You must have recorded timings, *see Record Narration* or *Timed Slideshow*): Slide Show>Set Up Show & /Browsed at a kiosk, /ok (Now when you run your show it will repeat itself over again).

Look Up Words – using Microsoft's internet references i.e. dictionary, encyclopedia, thesaurus etc:

| Mouse Click / | To > | Task Pane TP |

Right /any word in your presentation>Look Up, & look for the results displayed in TP

Password – allowing users to "Read only" your presentation, not modify it without a password, or not view it at all without a password: Tools>Options, /Security *tab* & in "Password to open" type a **password**, (or to allow users, who you don't want to modify your presentation, but to "Read only" your presentation, type a **password** in "Password to modify" *box* instead) /ok, type it again, /Save (Note: you could add different passwords to both "to open" & "to modify" *boxes*, but when the user opens your presentation they'll have to enter the "Password to open" password, & then either /Read only (b) they'll have your 2nd password to enter and get past the "Read only" to modify your presentation. 2nd Note: the "Read only" means the user is not only unable to make change to your presentation, but in addition they can't copy parts of it to paste it in another, or perform as Save As at all!) To delete the password: Open your presentation & enter correct password(s) & Tools>Options & delete password(s).

Insert Comments – like sticky notes, you can insert a comment to yourself or others in design view of your presentation: Insert>Comment & type a **comment**, /off in blank area. Hover over note for pop-up, or / & drag note anywhere on slide, //Note to reopen & edit.

Merge & Review – To merge many different presentations into your original, & then accepting or rejecting any part of the merged images, text etc. For example, you want to email a few of your friends: Shaggy & Daphne, a copy of your presentations, asking them to make changes to it, and then send them back to you where you can merge both of theirs into your original where you'll read & either accept or reject their changes one at a time:

1. You – File>Save As & name first one **Shaggy**, & save a copy for **Daphne** as well, and then email them or put them on a disk & hand it to them.
2. Editor (s) – Shaggy & Daphne will open their presentations & make changes, /Save & either email or hand your disk back to you with their saved changes.
3. You – Put both Daphne & Shaggy's presentations on your computer's Desktop, open your "original" version & Tools>Compare & Merge Presentations, browse to your Desktop & select Daphne & Ctrl+/ Shaggy's presentations (to select both), /Merge (b), /Continue…
    a. TP: /Reviewers *arrow* & uncheck Daphne (so all we see are tags of "Shaggy's" changes in the presentation. Note: Depending on the name of the computer Shaggy or Daphne edited their copies of your presentation on, is the name you'll see here. In other words, if both of them edited their copies on "YOUR" computer, then the Reviewer names will be the same "YOUR NAME"), /off in blank area…
    b. TP: under "Slide changes" select 1 & over on slide check its corresponding box to accept changes…
On TP you can /Gallery *tab* (to view full slide views of changes), & when you're done accepting or rejecting all the changes, on Review *toolbar* /End Review (b)

Format Bullets – To change your bullets to a picture: Select your bullets on a slide & Right / them>Bullets & Numbering, /Picture (b) & /on a picture once, /ok

Button (b)	Enter or Return ®	Close X

Shortcuts

Esc *key* – Press Esc *key* to end Slide Show
F4 – Like Format Painter, *but* it only applies *most recent* action or formatting performed.
F5 – View Slide Show
F7 – Spell checks to entire presentation
Cntrl+Home – Puts cursor at the very beginning of the slides.
Cntrl+End – Puts cursor at the very end of the slides.
Home – Puts cursor at beginning of a line.
End – Puts cursor at end of line.
Tab – in Outline *view* will demote a slide to a bullet
Shift+Tab – in Outline view will promote a bullet to a slide
Ctrl+A – Selects *all*.
Ctrl+Z – Undo any action
Ctrl+Y – Redo any undid action.
Ctrl+S – Save
Ctrl+X – Cut
Ctrl+T – Font window
Ctrl+V – Paste
Ctrl+F – Find
Ctrl+P – Print
Ctrl+D – Duplicate slide (Note: if an object is selected & you Ctrl+D it creates a duplicate of that object)
Ctrl+/ & Drag an object or some selected text to create a copy of it

Slide Show Shortcuts – Use following during your slide show presentation:
Press 8® (to go to slide 8)
Press W (White out)
Press B (Black out), press B again & slide reappears
Right /slide>Pointer Options>Pen (press ESC to exit pointer)
Press E (erases)
Press N (next slide)
Press H (if the next slide is hidden, press H to reveal it)
Hold both mouse buttons down for about 2 seconds (computer beeps) and you go back
to slide one.
Press F1 (view shortcuts)

| Mouse Click / | To > | Task Pane TP |

Access

Overview

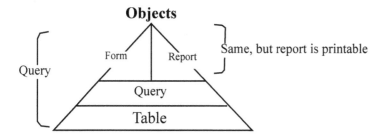

Form = Displays data from tables or queries; or enter new data
Report = print results of forms or queries
Query = to retrieve data from a table
Table = raw organized data

Create Database – The Database is the Access software program you create to store your tables in – tables are the foundation in the Access Database upon which ALL data is extracted and used by other Objects like Queries, Forms and Reports: Open Access & in <u>TP</u> /Blank Database *link*, type the **name** of your database, choose a place you'd like to store your data, & /Create (b). Next: *see Normalized*

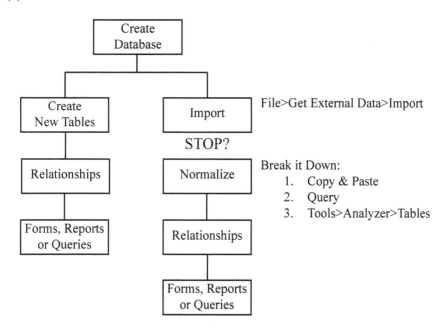

Tables – Are like Excel Spreadsheets in that they will have many cells for you to create & store your records in. Don't create one table to store all your information as its inefficient i.e. say you're searching the internet for paint. Do you want over one million results? That would be information overload, but instead you break down what you want in your search and the same goes for creating tables, create them with the smallest most meaningful data. In other words, a table should contain information only on one subject i.e. a Personal table, Benefits table, Orders table, Shipping table, Customers table, Vendors table, Manufacturers table etc. If you create a table that contains all your data, and you want only to look up a customer, you'll have to wait and wait as your table pulls in not only your customer info, but everything else you don't care to view – slows down processing time immensely. But don't worry you do have the option later to pull up a customer from a customer table along with his order from your order table, *see Relationships*:

Normalized Tables – A table is normalized when each field contains smallest, meaningful value & contains no repeating groups; break them apart if they do (Note: It would be a lot easier if you create your tables first with this in mind so you don't have to break any tables down later, as it's strongly recommended because smaller tables are easier to maintain and make the database run extremely more efficiently). For an example, let's say you have a table dedicated strictly for Clients and you have the following fields in the table:

1. Name – Is not the smallest, meaningful value. Break name down into two *fields*:
    a. First Name
    b. Last Name
2. Address – Break address down into four *fields*:
    a. Street
    b. City
    c. State
    d. Zip
3. Email Address – This is tricky, because some clients may have more than one email address. It might be better to create another table dedicated to email addresses: *see Tables*

Create Tables, in Design View – Tables are like Excel Spreadsheets in that they will have many cells for you to create & store you records in: In your Database under "Objects" select "Tables" & in its adjacent *window* //Create Table in Design View…(Note: After you create all your tables: *see Keys*). Each Table has basically 2 views; one is the Design View to create titles for each field you'd like to see in your record i.e. First Name, Last Name, City, Street, Phone etc.

Field Name – To name the field i.e. First Name, Last Name or whatever…

Data Type – Specifies the data stored in a table field;

- Text – Will store both numbers & text in this field, but no calculations can be performed for this field
- Memo – Stores more characters than the Text Data type
- Number – Use this Data Type for fields you'd like later to perform calculations

Mouse Click /	To >	Task Pane TP

with like cost, gross pay, employees hours
- AutoNumber – Is used for numbering your records, a unique identifier for each record
- Yes/No – A box will display that you can check after you change to your datasheet view that you can check like do your records have health insurance check yes or leave blank for no
- Lookup Wizard – creates drop down arrow in the specified *field* of your Table's Datasheet View that a Data Enterer can / on to pull-up its details i.e. if you have Department Code *field* in your Employees *table* that is based on codes like HR, PR, TW…and a new user doesn't know what these codes mean, and would have to open the Department Names Table to lookup the full name for the code, you can cut that step out and have the user remain in the Employees table. The trick is to link the codes from the Department Names *table* to this table, through which the full name will be available to the user without ever having to open up the Department Names *table* through using the Lookup Wizard (Note: you don't need another table for to create a lookup field *see Lookup Field*): Data Type *arrow>* Lookup Wizard, /Next & select a table you have codes and their full names in (this example Department Names), /Next & //the fields to add them to your "Selected Fields" (Note: it would be helpful to add both the code field and the code's full name field so user can reference both), /Next, & /Sort *arrow>*a field you'd like to sort by if any, /Next uncheck "Hide Key Column" (this will display the Primary Key Code *field* in the lookup), expand Department Name column to see full names by / & drag the right most edge of it's shaded gray heading bar (your pointer will turn into a two-way arrow when it's right over the edge, then / & drag or //it really fast & like Excel, it will automatically adjust the column to the longest text of that column), /Next (select the field that is the Unique Identifier, typically the field with the Primary key *see Table Keys*), /Next & type a **name**, /Finish, /Yes, /Datasheet View (b) & /in Department Code *cell* & an *arrow* will appear, /that *arrow>*your list.
  - Column Headings – You can now add headings for both columns: /in Dept Code *field* & down below in Field Properties, /Lookup *tab* & //Column Heads *cell>*Yes, /Datasheet View (b) & /in Department Code *field* to see headings…
  - Column Widths – if your columns are too small then: /in Dept Code *field* & below in its Field Properties, /Lookup *tab* & /in Column Widths & change the 1st column>**1** or **2** inches (1st column is the first # on the left-side of the semi-colon).
- Lookup Field – creates drop down arrow in the specified *field* of your Table's Datasheet View that a Data Enterer can / on to pull-up its details without linking to another table: /in Health Insurance *field* (as an example) & down below in Field Properties, /Lookup *tab* & /in Display Control *cell*, /it's *arrow>*Combo Box ® & /Row Source Type *arrow>*Value List ® & type your values separated by commas i.e. **Yes, No, Maybe, Don't Bother Me** ® (Note: Make sure Column Count *cell* reads "1" column & not 2), /Save, /Datasheet View (b) & /in a Health Insurance *cell* & an *arrow* will appear, /that *arrow>*your list.

Description – Here you can type in a detailed description of what each field is for & how it's to be used.

Button (b)	Enter or Return ®	Close X

<u>Field Properties</u> – Used to refine what and how data can be entered into your fields: After you've typed in your field name & selected a Data Type, press F6 to toggle down to its Field Properties (Note: pressing F6 again will take from you back from properties to its *field*)…

> <u>Validation Rule</u> – To limit data being entered into a field i.e. **<30** (only values less than 30 are accepted) OR **<=**30 (Less than OR equal to 30, and know that the equals sign comes ALWAYS at the left of a < or > sign or you'll get an error!)
>
> > <u>Validation Text</u> – here you can type **error message** that will appear if Data Enterer enters a # out of the range you set in the *Validation Rule*
>
> <u>Required</u> – set this field to yes and the Data Enterer won't be able to leave this *field* blank, but will be forced to enter data for this particular *field* before saving the record: //Required *field* (//some fields will toggle them between choices & in this case "yes" or "no")
>
> <u>Default Value</u> – Enter a value you want as a default for this field every time you start a new record i.e. 40 for the average employee hired by your company; as default you won't have to type 40.
>
> <u>Input Mask</u> – Symbols to define to user amount of characters needed i.e. (###) ###-### (Like a phone #): /in Input Mask's *cell* of your Phone's *field* property & /its Build (b) (it will look like three little dots …) & follow the directions (Note: the last step of the wizard will ask about choosing to store with or without symbols, if you choose without the symbols, the symbols will still be displayed to the user but won't store them and hence will reduce the size of your database)
>
> > <u>Custom Mask</u> – to create a custom mask i.e. a Product ID for each one of our 21 varied Chocolate with Nuts products, so the ID could be **CHN1-19** where CH is abbreviation for Chocolate and N for nuts and then 1-19 as an added identifying #: /Input Mask's *cell* of your Product ID's *field* property & /it's Build (b), /Edit List (b) & /New (b) (has * asterisk) & in Description type **Product ID** ®, Input Mask: **!LLL0-00** ® (Note: Exclamation point starts the programming and after it are L's that allow text to be entered in this field for text & 0's for #'s), ® type _ ,® **CHN1-01** (you have to enter Sample Data), /Close, /Next, /Next & select with or without symbols, /Next, /Finish
>
> <u>Help</u> – Press **F1** on your keyboard when your cursor is in any *field* in Design view to bring up details and definitions of what that field.

Datasheet View, Entering Records – After you've created your fields for your data to be entered into, then change your view to enter in those fields the info that will make up each record: On *toolbar* /Datasheet (b). Remember if you need to go back & make Design changes to your table on toolbar /Design View (b)

> <u>Entering Data</u> – To create a new record: /in the 1st blank *cell* of the last and only blank row & start typing. To save a record: move into another record or hold SHIFT+® (Note: closing the table after making changes to a record without saving the record first, will ironically still be saved, but it's good measure to get into the habit of seeing it saved yourself). To delete a record: /anywhere in the row of the record you want deleted and on

Mouse Click /	To >	Task Pane <u>TP</u>

toolbar /Delete Record (b). If stuck with data entry: always press ESC once or twice.

Record Navigating Bar – You can use your mouse or arrow keys to move from one record to the next, but don't forget at the bottom of your table you also have a Record Navigation Bar (Also found in most other object like at the bottom of Forms):

These 2 arrows advance 1
record at a time

|◀ ◀ [   ] ▶ ▶| ▶ ✳ { New Record (b)

These 2 arrows take you
directly to the first or last
record in your table

Filter & Sorting Records – To filter out unwanted records for a time without deleting them, and then bringing them back when desired.

Sorting Records – / in a *column* you'd like your records sorted by i.e. Last Name & on *toolbar* /desired sort (b) Ascending or Descending

Filter By Form – On *toolbar* /Filter By Form (b) (Note: all your data will be temporarily hidden), /in a empty *cell* i.e. under the *column* heading named "State", & /its *arrow*>a name of a state **UT**, on *toolbar* /Apply Filter (b). You can add more to your first filter "UT" by /Filter By Form (b) again, & at the bottom, lower-left corner of your *screen*, /Or tab, /in a empty *cell* i.e. under the *column* *heading* named "Country", & /its *arrow*>**Germany**, *toolbar* /Apply Filter (b) (Note: As in Queries, anything in the "or" (Over Ride) *cell* or in this case in the OR *tab*, is not bound by any criteria)

Filter By Selection – To do quick filter by what you have selected i.e. you're in the "State" *column* & in the field that contains UT for Utah, & you want to only see all records containing UT: Right /that UT *cell*>Filter By Selection. To remove you filter: Right /anywhere in the table>Remove Filter Sort

Filter Excluding Selection – To filter OUT or remove all fields that you've selected: If you're in the "State" *column* for your records & you want to view all records excluding NY (New York) Right /the cell that contains NY in *any* record>Filter Excluding Selection. To remove you filter: Right /anywhere in the table>Remove Filter Sort

Remove Filter Sort – After, Sorting, Filtering by either Selection or Excluding, to revert your table back to its original view: Right /any cell>Remove Filter Sort

Advanced Filter Sort – Record>Filter>Advanced Filter Sort & in Field List (a small box floating at top of your *window* that is displaying the names of all your *fields* from your table this Filter is based upon, using the Query) & //a *field* from the Field List to add it to the *grid* below & then in it's Criteria *cell* type a **criteria** (for a list *see Advanced Criteria* under *Query*), on *toolbar* /Apply Filter (b) ... /Remove Filter (b) to undo your filter

| Button (b) | Enter or Return ® | Close X |

Keys – after you've created your tables and have them normalized the next step is to add a Primary Key (or an additional *field* you designate as a Primary Key) and a Foreign Key *field* to each table in order to *link* (or create relationships) between tables. Without links between tables you wouldn't be able to pull up related data and hence would have to put all your data into one table, but that's extremely inefficient. When you are finished with establishing fields in your tables as Primary or Foreign Keys: *see Relationships.*

Primary Key – is a *field* you designate that uniquely identifies a record and:
1. that Primary Key *field* never contains blank values
2. doesn't allow duplicates

For example: you have an Employees *table* that includes the *fields*: Hire Date, Phone, First and Last names. Which *field* would uniquely identify each employee? It couldn't be First Name, because some employees may have same first names. The best thing to do is create an additional *field* named **Employee ID** in the Table's Design View & on *toolbar* /Primary Key (b) to make it the Primary Key *field*, and be sure in Datasheet View, # the employees or use their Social Security #s, as the SS# will never be duplicates.

Foreign Key – is the field you designate in one table that will have the same Data Type *value* as the Primary *key* of another table, and then you can open the Relationship *window*, and *link* the *fields* together.

For example: You've already created an Employee ID *field* in your Employee *table* and assigned it a Primary *key*. But you also have an Employees Personal *table* that includes the *fields*: Emergency Contact, Home Address, Home City, Home State, Home Zip Code and Home Phone. None of these *fields* have the same Data Type as the designated Primary *key field* in Employees *table*. Create another *field* in Employees Personal *table* called EMPID (Note: it can be the same name as the Primary Key *field* "Employee ID," but I find it easier to keep track of Foreign and Primary *keys* if I abbreviate the Primary Keys name as the name for my Foreign *key* field, hence EMPID) or EMP ID for short) & make sure its "Data Type" is the exact same as the Primary *key field* in Employees *table* (except if Primary *key's* Data Type is "AutoNumber" then the Foreign *key's* Data Type will be "Number." Note: even though no *fields* of First or Last Names are in Employees Personal *table*, remember, you won't need them when you can *link* the two tables together and be able to pull those *fields* in!)

Relational Database – Access is a relational database meaning it can pull related information from more than one related table. To identify table relationships in your database, if any: *Toolbar* /Relationships (b)

Primary Key – required to create a relational database, and will appear bold in the relationship *window*

Foreign Key – is the field that the primary *key* is related to and linked to and seen in this window as not bold, but a line connecting it to the bold text (Primary Key) of another table

Multiple Primary Keys – a table can have more than one primary key (more than one

Mouse Click /   To >   Task Pane <u>TP</u>

bold text in a table in the relationship *field*) and can relate to other primary keys

Subdatasheets – Can only be viewed in the Datasheet *view* of your Table, if prior, you've or somebody else created a relationship with this table to another, *see Relationships*: At the beginning of each record you'll see a + sign, / it to expand that record's to view its related record from its other related table. (Note: if you have a table related to a table, related to a third table you can insert a Subdatasheet inside an already expanded Subdatasheet to view the 3rd related table: Expand the first Subdatasheet then Insert> Subdatasheet, select the name of the table that is related to your 1st Subdatasheet (table). To close the Subdatasheets: Format>Subdatasheet>Remove)

Relationships – After finishing creating your tables and establishing Primary and Foreign Keys in each one, next is getting those tables to interact by hooking up similar values & Data Type fields between them (Remember, putting all of your information into one table is inefficient and slows down your processing speed).

Build – *toolbar* find and /Relationships (b), & add whatever tables to the tan *window* that you want to form relationships between. Then /& drag one field name from one table to another (Again, both fields must have same Data Type & Properties. Note: The text in bold in each table is the Primary Key; and typically you'll drag this field over & onto another table that has a Foreign Key – if you followed Dream Notes 2003 in setting up your table's Keys, then the Foreign Key is the field that is an abbreviated name of your Primary Key that isn't bold in your second table); after hooking them up you'll have a *window* pop-up with a few options to check:

✓ Enforce Referential Integrity – Check this box, because without it you could create "Orphan" *records*. Orphans are records that don't have a corresponding record in the 'Initiator' or 'Primary' table, and hence will produce inaccurate results every time you query a table that contains Orphan records. But checking this box alone will prevent you from adding, deleting or changing ANY records including ALL tables it's related to. So check also the Cascade options…

    o Side note: the only time you may NOT want to enforce a relationship is when you have a relationship between the tables that would require each record in the 1st *table* to have a corresponding record in the 2nd *table* i.e. your Employees *table* is linked to the Employees Website *table* and since not every employee has their own personal website it wouldn't work well to check Enforce at all & try to require data from the 2nd table that may have blank cell, but of course you don't have to create a that 2nd table at all for notes, and that would be called *Denormalizing*…

    o Denormalization – NOT putting a *field* that may contain occasional blanks or empty data into a table of its own i.e. Leaving a Website Address *field* in with the Employees Table, instead of creating its own solitary table name "Client Website Addresses", and *linking* it to the Clients Table (Because not all Clients may have Websites you will end up with some blanks sooner or later, so some experts say it's better to normalize the field into its own table, but it's not a set rule)

✓ Cascade – Check the 2 Cascade options, and they will allow you to later

Button (b)	Enter or Return ®	Close X

update & modify records in related tables, but when making changes ALWAYS start with the 'Initiator' table 1ˢᵗ *see 1 to 1 or 1 to many.* By also starting with the 'Initiator' first, its corresponding linked key fields with other tables will update themselves automatically too.

Edit – To Edit or delete a relationship // the thin line connecting the related tables & make your changes

1-to-1 – After you create a relationship and notice it's a one-to-one relationship, it's important to remember the 1ˢᵗ table you dragged your field from (the Initiator of the relationship) that created the relationship with the other table, because later when you want to add, delete or make any changes with the records in the two tables, Access only allows changes to be made in the 'Initiator' table FIRST. After, you can add, delete or change records in the 2nd related table.

1-to-Many – If your relationships between tables is a one to many then it's important later when you want to add, delete or make any changes with the records in the tables to start with the table that is labeled the '1' relationship & then after you can make changes with its related "Many" table

Many-too-Many – is something that Access doesn't compute. Either normalize your tables or create a separate codependent table that has both Primary and Foreign Key fields of both tables that you want to link together, and let this third table be the unhealthy go between, which will wind up having a 1-to-Many relationship with the two tables.

Import Excel – File>Get External Data>Import, browse & change your File Type> Microsoft Excel, find & //your Excel file & follow the wizard.

Export to Excel – Select your table first & then File>Export & change your File Type> Microsoft Excel 97-2003 & pick a place to export your table to & /Export (b)

Backup – to back up a table: Right /table desired to be backed up>Copy, then Right /white space in Database>Paste & select & type new name for the Table & select a type…
- Structure Only – paste's only the fields of a copied table
- Structure & Data – paste's the fields & their data into a new table
- Append Data to Existing Table – here you type in the name of an existing table you'd like to paste (append) the data you've copied from the other table. (The field names need to be the same when appending too)

Reset AutoNumber – When your records in a Table are uniquely defined by AutoNumber & you delete one, AutoNumber does not automatically renumber itself & you're left with # gaps i.e. 1, 2, 4, 5, 9, 10 etc. The following steps will show you how to reset AutoNumber for a table that has one reference (or one relationship to one table). If there is more than one table referenced, you'll have to repeat these steps for each referenced table:
1. Delete the relationships between tables.
2. Main Table –
   a. Change the "Data Type" of your AutoNumber *field* in your main table

to Number & then remove the Primary Key, /Save (you MUST /Save before proceeding!)

    b. Create a new AutoNumber *field* & name it **Main Table Field**, /Save, & close the table.

3. <u>Referenced Table</u> –

    a. Open up your table that your main table will be referenced to, & create a new Number *field* & Title it **Referenced Table Field**, & save it, & close the table.

4. <u>Update Query</u> – We need to create an Update Query that updates the new *field* in your referenced table to the new AutoNumber *field* in your main table

    a. Create a query in Design view

    b. Add your two tables, Main & Referenced

    c. Find the field in your Main *table* that was previously linked to the Reference *table* & drag to re-link those fields together to create a join.

    d. On *toolbar* /the *arrow* to the right of the Query Type (b)>Update Query

        i. //referenced *field* titled "Referenced Table Field" (to add it to grid below)

        ii. In its Update To *cell* type 2 sets of brackets: in the first set will be the name of your main table, & in 2nd pair of brackets the name of your new AutoNumber *field* of your main table i.e. if your main table's name was "Candy" & the new AutoNumber field in that table is titled "Main Table Field," type **[Candy].[Main Table Field]** (this syntax will update the new field values in the referenced table).

        iii. Run the Query & /Yes to update # row(s)

        iv. File>X & /No to save.

5. Delete the "original" linking *field* from your main table & the referenced table.

6. Rename the *new* AutoNumber *field* to "original" name

7. Re-create the primary key & the relationship between tables

Table Analyzer – helps to create new tables from an improperly designed one that already contains data. The Analyzer will eliminate repeating info in same fields by placing them in 2 or more related tables & can only be run on 1 table at a time: Select your table & Tools>Analyze>Table, /Next, /Next, /Next, /Next & move tables around so you can see them. If you like & agree with the "Analyzer" then rename the tables: select a table & /Rename Table (b) & type in a name, /ok & finish naming the rest, /Next, /Next, /Next, /Yes & make sure "No, don't create query" is selected & uncheck "Display help…", /Finish, /ok

Many-To-Many Relationships – Access does not support them. For example: to create a many-to-many relationship between two tables is to create a relationship between the two without "Enforce Referential Integrity," but that's not all, the table's Main *field* would typically have no Primary Keys (as a result contain annoying duplicate records) and hence the messy result is a many-to-many relationship between Table's 1 & 2. If your tables do have these symptoms, it's best to create an intermediary (or junction) 3rd Table, in which you will add 1 *field* from Table's 1 & 2 (those Main *fields* may have duplicates, but will be the one that you will want to have no duplicates in; considered to be Primary Keys – at this point you'll only be considering); hence you want to have the 3rd table be the

Button (b)	Enter or Return ®	Close X

junction table that will establish a one-to-many relationships with the other 2 tables:

1. Create 3rd Table – create a new 3rd table containing the 1 Main *field* from each of the two tables with the exact same: Name, Data Type & Field Property of what you consider to be the Primary Key *fields* of the other 2 tables (only considering now, because later you'll fix Tables 1 & 2's Main *fields* to be Primary Keys, but since they have duplicate records Access would have a hissy fit if you tried to set those Main *fields* to be unique by assigning them the Primary Key now). Make those 2 *fields* in your new table both Primary Keys & Save & X the table

2. Add Records to 3rd Table – Next, you'll want to copy (append) the records from one of the 2 tables to your 3rd Table: //Create Query in Design & add 1 of the 2 tables involved in the many-to-many relationship, & lets call it **Table 1**. Add 2 *fields*, the *fields* that you would consider to be the Primary Key *field* & the Foreign Key *field* (the *field* that is either linked to Table 2's Main *field* right now in the many-to-many relationship, or the name of the other field in the 2nd table that is linked to your Main *field* in Table 1) to the Query grid below. On *toolbar* /the *arrow* to the right of the Query Type (b)>Append Query, & /Table Name *arrow*> your 3rd table, /X, /Run, /Yes (This error is because Table 1 has duplicates, which is a violation to append to Table 3 because of the <u>Primary keys</u> that won't allow duplicates. So duplicate records won't append), /Yes & X Query without saving.

3. Restructuring Tables 1 & 2 – Next, to restructure the 2 tables into 2 new tables so as to comply with the 3rd intermediary table's design – removing duplicate fields from the 2 tables: Right /Table 1> Copy, Right /a blank area in your Database>Paste & type new *temporary* name for the restructuring of Table 1 i.e. **Table1Temp** & select "Structure Only," /ok…
   - Structure Only – paste's only the fields of a copied table
   - Structure & Data – paste's the fields & their data into a new table
   - Append Data to Existing Table – here you type in the name of an existing table you'd like to paste (append) the data you've copied from the other table. (The field names need to be the same when appending too)
   Right /Table 2>Copy, Right /white blank space in your Database>Paste & type **Table2Temp** & select "Structure Only," /ok

4. Remove Foreign Key Fields – Now you'll delete the 1 Foreign Key *field* in each of your new "Temp" Tables (Because those Foreign Keys will both be new Primary Keys in the 3rd Table that will link or relate to the Main Fields in Tables 1 & 2). Now make your Main Fields what you consider to be Primary key fields in your TempTables 1 & 2 & make them Primary Key fields.

5. From Original>TempTables – Next, is to copy the records out of the original tables & paste them into their corresponding TempTables 1 & 2, using Append Query: //Create Query in Design, Add Table 1 to Query. Add all the *fields* from Table 1 into the Query grid, /Query Type *arrow*>Append Query, /Table Name *arrow*>Temp1Table, /ok, /Run, /Yes, /Yes, X query & don't save. Repeat the same steps to add all records from Table 2>Table2Temp

6. Delete Old & Rename New Tables – Now that you've appended all the records from the old tables into your 2 new TempTables, you can delete the original tables. After original tables are deleted, Right /each TempTable>Rename & name

| Mouse Click / | To > | Task Pane <u>TP</u> |

them as the previously, original tables were named

7. <u>Relationships</u> – /Relationships (b) & Add Tables 1, 2 & 3 & put 3 in the middle & appropriately create the relationships and "Enforce Referential Integrity" too.

Linked Tables – This will insert a copy of a table from another database into your database & this table will be linked, so any changes made to it's origin table will be updated in its copy: In Database 1, File>Get External Data>Link Tables, //Database 2.mdb, select a Table, /ok (note: an *arrow* will appear left of table icon to show you it's *linked*)

Export To Outlook, Contacts, Using Smart Tags – Right /your Contacts *table*>Design View, /in Contact Name *field*, press F6 (Field Properties), /in Smart Tag *cell*, /its Build (b), check "Person Name," /ok, /View (b)>Datasheet View, /Yes (to save *table*), /In a Contact Name *field*, /it's Smart Tag>Add to Contacts, add more info to your contact including an email address & /Save & X (b). (Note: to edit data after you've X your contact, /on same Smart Tag>Open Contact or to send Email)

Mailing Labels – Create mailing labels from your table using wizard: Under "Objects" select Report & above "Objects" is the Database *toolbar*, /New (b) & select Label Wizard & /Table *arrow*> a table that contains your clients name, address, city, state etc. & add those *fields* & follow rest of wizards steps.

Merge with Word – to use "Office Links" to share data from Access with Word when doing a Mail merge: Under "Objects" select your table or query you'd like that data to be used in Word's Mail Merge & Tools>Office Links>Merge with Word, /ok, browse & find your form letter & //it. TP, /Next & /so your cursor is on 2nd line of page & on Mail Merge *toolbar* /Insert Merge Field (b) & //the fields you'd like to add to your form letter & close Field List when finished. TP, /Next, /Next & /Edit *link* to edit letters individually…

Update Links – to check that your tables are linked to correct source: Tools>Database Utilities> Linked Table Manager, /Select All (b), check "Always prompt for new location," /ok, //database.mdb, /ok

Store Pictures – How to store a different picture for each record
1. In your table create a *field* title 'Picture' & / its Data Type arrow>OLE Object
2. /View (b) (to go to Datasheet View) & / in the Picture's *field* or *cell* of the record, & Insert>Object & browse to find & insert your picture. Now go to record two's Picture *field* & Insert>Object & browse to find & insert your picture (continue this for each record you'd like a picture for. Note: There will be no actual pictures in these fields, they will come later when you view these fields in a Form.
3. Close Table
4. Open Form -
   a. Create a Form based upon your table that includes your Picture *field* & then…
   b. On Toolbox /Image (b) and then in your form's field list, / & drag the field you

Button (b)	Enter or Return ®	Close X

created in your table for the pictures, on to your Form, and you're done!

Query – If you are looking for a particular record(s) and don't have the time to scroll through your table of 100's or even 1000's of records you can use the Query to get precise results out of your tables. *Toolbar* /View (b) (Datasheet) to view result of your query & /View (b) (Design), again work on the Design of your query.

> Query Wizard – to create a query from a table or multiple tables: Under Objects /Query (b), //Create Query in Design View, a list of all your tables will pop-up so /Tables Queries *arrow*>(Yes you can base queries on other queries not just tables) a table and />> *arrows* (b) to move ALL available *fields* over (you can then select another table & />> again to add more data from another table to your Query) & follow the rest of wizard to complete your Query (Note: the Wizard will add all the fields from your tables to the queries grid, but if your query is based upon two or more related tables then only some of the fields from the tables will be added to the query's grid below)
>
> Criteria – Type in the Criteria *cell* of your corresponding field(s) the text you want an exact match for: For example, if I wanted to pull only those records that are from Utah, I would enter in its Criteria cell UT (or Utah, depending when you created your table if you had spelled it out or not). When finished on *toolbar* /Run (b) or the Datasheet (b) to see results.
>
>> Advanced – Advanced Criteria you can use in your queries:
>> - **<=30**   (Desired result to be less than or equal to 30)
>> - **>=40**   (Greater than or equal to 40)
>> - **30< And <40** (#'s greater than 30 &less than 40)
>> - **UT Or ID** (To see only Utah & Idaho clients)
>> - **<4/12/03** (All dates older than April 12, 2003)
>> - **m*** (The asterisk is a 'wild card.' Anything that stars with the letter M)
>> - **Is Null** (Looking for fields that have no values)
>
> (Warning! Any changes you make on the record in the Datasheet view i.e. changing a name from Bobby to Bob will be updated in the table, BUT if you delete a record in the query it won't delete it from the tables, unless you change your query from a Select Query>a Delete Query *see Delete Query*).
>
> Or – Anything in the "or" field is not bound by the any Criteria: For example, if you did a query with the criteria's – UT & >$50,000 (All Utah client's earning more than $50 thousand, & you decided you'd like to include in your criteria Idaho): Type ID in the 'or' field & it will pull up ALL Idaho clients irregardless of your $50,000 criteria.
>
> Calculating – Right /a blank Field *cell*>Build, / = (b), and in the middle column, // the field you want to add to the equation, / * (b) (asterisk to multiply), // your 2nd *field* name you want multiplied with the first field & /ok i.e. = **[WeeklyHours]*[HourlyRate]**. To change the Name of your new field: select in that cell 'Expr 1' and replace it with **Weekly Gross**.

Query Joins – Displaying two or more tables in a query and creating temporary joins: by / & dragging one field from one table to another field that contains the same value in the other table (just like creating relationships). By default created joins are Inner Joins. Warning! 2 or more tables not joined in a query will always give you bogus data. (Note: If you get an error from trying to open a query it's because there's two or more table listed in that query that

| Mouse Click / | To > | Task Pane TP |

aren't yet related, instead, Right /the query>Design View).

Inner Join – Displays only records from "both" tables that have matching values in the "joined fields"

Outer Join – To display all records from one table & only the matching records of the 2nd table i.e. After you have created a join, // that thin line (join) between the 2 tables and select #'s 2 or 3 according to their explanations and your desired results.

Self Join – To join a table to itself i.e. if you have an employee table that includes a column for Managers, and you want to display each employee with his Manager: Display the same Employee table twice and join from one table's *Employee ID* to it's duplicate table's, *Managers ID* (Note: you can't match a field from 1st table to same field of 2nd table, or id to id, it would be like a snake eating its tail and you'd get errors. Manager id has same value as Employee id but can be joined because they're separate fields in the table). To avoid confusion change the name of the table that has the Employees ID *field* (that is joined to the other table's Managers ID) by Right /it>Properties & in alias type **Managers** ® & X Properties. Then add the Last Name *fields* from both Employee & Manager *tables* to the *grid* below. Now in the grid find & /in the Last Name field, then Right /it>Properties & in Caption type **Managers** ® (This will have the Column Heading as Managers in Datasheet View) & X Properties & Run Query

3 Table Join – If you want to join two tables but they have no matching fields & values, you can bring in a 3rd table that can link or bridge the two through its matching fields with both tables.

Top Value Query – To query top 5 of anything i.e. sales people or products sold: *Toolbar* /Totals (b) (adds the Totals field to the *grid* below but as a "Group" for each field in the grid. It's best to only have 1 "Group," so all the others have to be changed>Sum or deleted from the Query). On *toolbar* /Top Values (Currently displaying the word "All") *arrow*>5 & Run Query

Omit Duplicate Records – If your query is pulling up duplicate records you can hide the extras, but this will only work if your records in your Datasheet View are exact duplicate copies in ALL *fields*, hence Duplicate records: In Design View, //top tan area, //Unique Records *cell*>Yes (Note: Unique Record is for entire record; Unique Value is to omit records with duplicate fields), X Properties

Parameter Query – Parameter Query's are nothing more than a prompt to the user (you) to type in an answer that will be used as criteria in your query every time you run it. For Example, if you only want to view clients from a particular state like Utah, in your query: Add that State *field* to the *grid* below & in its criteria *cell* type **[Enter a State]** Run your query & when prompted type in Utah, /ok. Other Parameter Queries include…

- Wildcards – Asterisks *, are used to abbreviate inquiries i.e. type in your criteria cell for your "State" *field* **Like [Enter the first letter of a State]&*** (the ampersand links parameter values to wildcard). So after you type in U for "Utah" & /ok your query will pull up all those states that begin with the letter "U"
- Between – Between, is used in a double parameter query to pull up #s or dates

| Button (b) | Enter or Return ® | Close X |

data between other #s or dates i.e. in your criteria *cell* of the Date *field* & type **Between [Enter a start date:] and [Enter an end date:]** (when you run your query this will ask the user the 2 questions above & as a result pull all the dates between what they entered in the start and entered in the end dates).

Update Query – To change values in a table with criteria you specify. For example, let's say we sell Licorice & it's time to update our prices by 5%: On *toolbar* /the *arrow* to the right of Query Type>Update Query (this puts an update *field* down in the *grid*), & in that *field* type in **[Licorice]*1.05** & *Toolbar* /Run (b) (Note: /View (b) won't run the query you have to /Run (b), & that's a nice safety option so you can view what you're going to update before running it), /Yes. (Note: If you run & Update, Append or a Delete Query on a table that you have open, the results won't show after your run the queries unless you close that table & reopen it, or Right /anywhere in your table>Remove Filter Sort)

Append Query – Used to add records from one table to another (Note: You must have matching *field* names & Data Type when appending from 1 table to another. If some fields don't match, then Access will ignore them and only append those that do): On *toolbar* /the *arrow* to the right of Query Type>Append, /Table Name *arrow*>a table you want the records added to & /ok, /Run, /Yes

Delete Query – To delete records from a table. First run your query to view the records you'd like to delete & then: /Query Type arrow>Delete Query, /Run, /Yes.

Publish to Excel – to publish a table or query to Excel to use special charting features Access doesn't have: Under Objects select your query & Tools>Office Links>Excel

Unmatched Query – A Query created to find if there are fields that aren't matched in another table; used to help find out what's missing in one table versus another, before merging the 2 tables together: Under "Objects," select Queries, & on Database *toolbar*, /New (b), //Find Unmatched Query Wizard, select **Table 1**, /Next, & select a table that contains related records (i.e. **Table 2**) /Next, select a *field* from both tables listed that have matching *fields* & in this case (Note: Matching *fields* typically don't have matching names, although that make sense & be easier) & then /<=> (b) /Next, & //Name of the *field* you chose earlier (to select the same *field* to appear in our Query results) /Next, /Finish (Hint: look at name of query in blue title bar. Also, Design View reveals an Outer Join, & an Is Null *criteria*)

Duplicate Query – A Query created to find duplicates and not add all those to the new table: Under "Objects," select Queries, & on Database *toolbar*, /New (b), //Find Duplicates Query Wizard, select **Table 1** /Next, //a *field* that might contain duplicate info /Next, /Finish (Note, Design View reveals the Totals (b) is used to group by name)

Query Criteria Groups & Summaries – how to Summarize records in the Criteria *field* with the added "Totals" *field* in your *grid* to "Group" *fields* by Products, Zip Codes etc.: In Design View of your Query on *toolbar* /Totals (b) to add Total *row* to your *grid* (Note: each *field* you may have previously in the *grid* will display the "Group" *text* in its Totals *cell*); which will group those fields together i.e. by State, then by Zip Code etc. – of course depending on

| Mouse Click / | To > | Task Pane <u>TP</u> |

which *field* is first, in the Query *grid,* will be the first field grouped. But what if we have formulas or Date *fields* in the *grid*? The "Group" *field* will have to be changed>"Expression" for your formula *fields* or "Where" for your Date *fields*. To summarize a *field* from same table or two different tables, after adding the "Totals" row to your *grid* i.e. /in a blank Field *cell* below in the *grid,* (The following formula is an example of the type of syntax you'd enter to summarize two fields i.e. Weekly Hours and Hourly Pay Rate to come up with Total Weekly Salary (TWS); from two different tables or from one table it's the same. The Query will figure out which table your *field* is calculating from as long as the two or more tables added to your Query don't have ANY fields with same names. Again, if you added the "Totals" *row* to the grid to Group your *field* like Customers together you'll have to change the Totals *cell* for any formulas from Group>Expression)

TWS: Sum([Weekly Hours]*[Hourly Rate])

(Note: anything in this formula that is on the left-side of the colon: is the name of the field, & on the right will be your syntax) To use a Date *field* with your Groups: add the "Date" *field* to the *grid* & again you'll have to /its Total *arrow* from Group>Where, then in its Criteria *cell* type a date i.e. **<5/1/04** (to find records Dated May 1, 2004 or earlier)

Crosstab Query – performs a summary calculation of intersecting values of row & column headings which are chosen by the user. Disclaimer: the following steps are general steps & are concepts because of the nature of what you choose, tables or queries & the fields you choose from them: Under "Objects" select Queries, then on Database's *toolbar* /New (b), select "Crosstab Query Wiz," /ok, select a table or query, /Next & select your fields, (you can specify here multiple row headings that will appear in columns at the left side of the crosstab), /Next (here you can only specify one that will appear at the top of each column) & select a value, /Next & select "Sum," (this can summarize the values in the rows & columns & are displayed in body of crosstab) /Next & /Finish

Pivot Table – to pivot (or filter) between data based on queries: Open your query & View>Pivot Table View & drag the fields from list onto desired Fields on table. To add more than 1 field to Detail Data field: select multiple fields from field list holding Shift *key* & at bottom of Field List *window* /its Row Area *arrow*>Detail Data, & /Add to (b).

Create New Field – To create a new field that multiplies or divides two fields: On *toolbar* /Calculated Totals & Fields (b)>Create Calculated Detail Field & in Name box type the name of your table & in *window* replace "0" with your syntax i.e. **hours*hourlyrate**, /Change (b), /Format *tab*, & /Number *arrow*>Currency

Total Sum – to get total sum of each *field* listed in your Rows Fields: /on your 1ˢᵗ column *heading* in your Detail Fields & on *toolbar* /AutoCalc (b) Σ>Sum

Details – to hide details from your Pivot Table: On toolbar /Hide Details (b). To see sub-detail fields & remove their parent details: In Detail Fields / + sign left of 1ˢᵗ column *heading* to expand, & once expanded you can see the sub-detail for that column, then you can / & drag its parent off on to *toolbars* above to remove it

Pivot Chart – to pivot (or filter) between data in a chart form, based on a query: Open your query & View>Pivot Chart View & drag the fields from list onto desired Fields on chart. After, you can change the structure of your chart by switching fields around by

| Button (b) | Enter or Return ® | Close X |

dragging them, or to remove them drag them off of chart

Sort – To sort data ascending or descending: Right /a Data Field's (b)>Sort>Descending

Chart Type – to change chart type i.e. pie>bar etc.: Right /white area>Chart Type: & select
another type of chart

Forms – Forms are another way creating or editing records in your tables, but in a format you decide from the structured tables.

AutoForm – Quickest way to create a Form from a table is: Select your Table & on *toolbar* /New Object AutoForm (b) (Note: some forms you create will automatically contain subforms, and it's because of the table your form is based upon relationship of one-to-many with other tables; a many-to-one won't create a default subform, nor will a one-to-one relationship), or use the...

Form Wizard – Under Objects /Forms, //Create Form by using Wizard, select a table and />> *arrows* (b) to move ALL available data over (you can then select another table & />>again to add more data from another table to your form) & follow the rest of wizard to complete your form. After you form is completed you'll be in the Form *view*...

Form View – In this view you can view your records from the table(s) & they will automatically be added (or updated) to the table when you make changes of your records in your new form: Bottom, lower-left of your form are some black triangles.

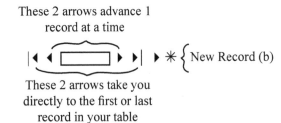

These 2 arrows advance 1 record at a time

These 2 arrows take you directly to the first or last record in your table

Design View – You can get to this view from your Form *view* up on *toolbar* /Design View (b) (To get back to Form view /Form View (b)), In this view just like in the Design view of your table you can make behind-the-scene changes to enhance the value & look of your form for other users including yourself...

Label – A Label does nothing more than places itself as a label next to a *field* (Called a Text Box) in your Form. To edit or change the name of your Label: //the Label & type your new text in.

Text Box – A box that displays the information from the fields of each record of the table your form was based off of i.e. Names, Addresses etc. (Note: the best way to tell the difference between a box that could be a Label or a Text Box, Right /it>Properties and look up on the Property's *window* blue bar and it will say):

Moving – To move a Text Box with its Label: /on either one and hover your mouse over it until you see a *hand* them / & drag the hand. For just moving the Label or Text Box individually: / on Label (or Text Box) and hover over upper-left corner of it till you see a *pointing finger*, then / & drag the finger.

Field List – The Field List is a floating box which lists all the fields from the table your Form is based on. If you accidentally delete a *field* on your form you can drag these names from the Field List onto the form (Note: if you don't have a field list that means either you haven't built your form using the wizard based off of your tables, or the Field List is hiding in which case up on the *toolbar* /Field List (b))

Header Footer – to add a header or footer to your form which text or pictures you put in them will stay static when user toggles through it's forms records: In Design View, View>Form Header Footer (Note: two bars will be added to your design *grid*, you move your pointer to the top edges of these bars and drag them up or down for sizing your Header or Footer space).

Pictures – To insert a picture into your form: In Design View, From floating *Toolbox*, /Image (b) & /on grid wherever you want your image, then browse & select your image

Combo Box – Create a drop down list of fields from your table: In Design View, On *Toolbox*, (On *Toolbox* make sure Control Wizards (b) is highlighted) & /Combo Box (b), & / on grid wherever you want your drop down list to go, /Next, select a table, /Next & select all the fields you want, /Next & /Sort *arrow*>a *field* you want to sort by, /Next & uncheck the Hide *box* & best fit the columns so all text can be seen, /Next, /Next & select Store That Value *arrow*>a key *field* (this is the main field – Key *field*, to store our value in), /Next, /Finish. Go to your Form *view* & test it!

Options – To add radial dials or options to your form. For example, you can have options for payments i.e. Credit Card, Check etc: In Design View, On *Toolbox* (make sure Control Wizards (b) is highlighted), /Option Group (b) & /on blank area of your form & type in the *labels*: **Credit Card** (press Tab *key*) **Money Order** (Tab) etc., ® & /Default *arrow*>Money Order, ® ® & /Store the value in this field *arrow*>the *field* you created earlier in a table this form is based upon i.e. Payment *field*, & finish the rest of the wizard. Test in Form *view*!

Command Button – To create a (b) on your form & assigning a function to it i.e. closing the form the (b) currently resides in or opening another form: In Design View, In floating *Toolbox*, /Command (b) & / anywhere on the form, & in left *window* pane select "Form Operations" & in right *pane* select "Close Form", /Next & select an option, /Next & title it, /Finish

Subform – Inserting one form into another, but 1st make sure forms are linked so all records displayed in subform are related to current record displayed in Main form, and it's nice too so you can view a record in one form & see its corresponding record in the subform. Also, although subforms resided inside Main form, they act both separate: On *toolbox* (Make sure Control Wizards (b) is highlighted) & /Subform (b), then / anywhere on the form: 1st Wizard asks you for a data source for the subform, so pick a tables (as one option) /Next, & /Tables Queries *arrow*>to a table that has a link relationship to this form that the table is based upon, then //The Tables *fields* to add them to your subform /Next, (you need to select one of the

| Button (b) | Enter or Return ® | Close X |

links Access suggests; this will link your form to your table you want as a subform, or create one of you own. It's important so that the subform displays info that corresponds appropriately to the main form i.e. Main form has your clients and you can create a subform of your Orders *table* that will list all of your clients orders!) /Next, & type in **name** of your Subform, /Finish & Test it!

Form Pivot Chart – to create a pivot chart in a form, based on a query: //Create Form by Using Wiz, & chose your query & add your fields, /Next & select Pivot Chart, /Next & select a style, /Next & type a name, /Finish & drag the fields from list onto desired Fields on chart. Next, open up a form in Design View that you'd like your Pivot Chart inserted as subform & on *toolbox* /Subform Subreport (b) & / in a blank area of grid & select "Use an existing form," & select your PivotChart Form you just created & /Next & select "Define My Own" & /Form Report *arrow*>a *field* you'd like linked to your chart so when you toggle through your records the chart will reflect those records, then /Subform Subreport *arrow*>same *field* name as you just selected so they're matching (In other words, you'll be matching Primary Key in the Form>Foreign or Primary Key in Subform) to *link* your form to your sub-form's Chart, /Next, /Finish

    Axis Titles – to change these title names: Right /an "Axis Title">Properties, /Format *tab* in Caption *box* replace text with a new name for Axis & close the box. Or you can delete these by selecting & hit Delete *key*

Macro, Button To Open Form – Macros are commands you create that can quicken your productivity. To create a macro to open a form: Under Objects /Macros & on Database *toolbar* /New (b), & /Action Cell's *arrow*>Echo, press F6 (to toggle to Echo's Properties) & /Echo>No (Echo No – won't show macro running in background, only its end results), /In 2nd Action Cells *arrow*>OpenForm, press F6, /Form Name's *arrow*>a form you'd like this macro to open, /Save & X Macro. To create a button for your macro...

    Add Button – to apply your "Open Form" macro to a (b) in a form: Open your form in Design view you'd like to create a (b) that will open up another form. On *toolbox* turn off "Wizard" with a /, & /Command (b) & add it to your form. Right /your new (b)>Properties & in Name Field replace text with new name, then /Event *tab*, in "On Click" *cell*, /its *arrow*>your Open Form macro made in the step above, then /its Build (b)... (which will open up the Open Form macro), /in Open Form *cell*, press F6 (takes your cursor to Properties) & /in "Where Condition" *cell* (this condition will compare a *field* in original form & find its match in 2nd form & bring up its complete record in the 2nd form – that is if you've created 2nd form containing the same field as your original form; this will happen after somebody hits your OpenForm (b)), Shift+F2 (to zoom) & type [Name of a *field* in your original form]=[Forms]![Formname i.e. Name of your 2nd form this form will be relating to]![Field Name of 2nd form i.e. name of other field that contains same data as field in 1st form], i.e. **[ClientID]=[Forms]![ClientDetails]![ClientID]** /Save & X Macro & test your (b)

Macro, Require Data Entry – checking the data entered & executing a macro i.e. if a *field* is left blank the record won't save, give you an error message & take you back to that blank *field* too: Open your form in Design View, Right /dark gray area>Properties (Form Properties), /Event *tab*, /in "Before Update" *box* (used to specify events that will occur before data in control is

Mouse Click /	To >	Task Pane TP

updated) & /its Build (b) …, select "Macro Builder," /ok & type **name** of your macro, /ok. On *toolbar* /Conditions (b) & in 2nd Condition *cell* type the Is Null expression of what *field* can't be blank i.e. **[ProductName] is Null** ® (this condition will run the macro if no value is entered in Product Name *field*) & / 2nd Action cell's *arrow*>CancelEvent ® In 3rd Condition *cell* type ... (Note: entering … or "ellipse" allows you to attach more than one condition) ®

> Create Message Error – /Action cell>MsgBox ® press F6 & type **You must enter a value in the Product Name field** ® ® & /Type *arrow*>Information ® **Required Data** In 4th Condition *cell* type ... ® & /4th Action cell's *arrow*> GoToControl ® & press F6 & type **[ProductName]** (In other words, when the record is not save because Product Name field was skipped this will Go back to Product Name field, Go To Control) ® & press F6 & type /Save & X Macro

Macro, Automate – A macro that enters a value in one field based upon a value in another field i.e. if someone enters the product name "Gummy Bears" then in another field you called, Gifts, you could have displayed "Free Shipping": Open your form in Design View, Right /Product text box>Properties, /Event *tab*, /in "On Exit" *field* & /its Build (b) ... & select "Macro Builder," /ok & type a name for your Macro, /ok, *toolbar* /Conditions (b) & /in 2nd Condition *cell* type **[Product] in ("Gummy Bears","Gummy Worms")** (this will compare values in this Product field with values in parenthesis) ® & / 2nd Action *arrow*> SetValue ® & type, press F6 & type **[Gifts]** (this is name of field), ®, & type **"Free Shipping"** (is the value you want displayed in the Gifts *field*). /in 3rd Condition *cell* & type ... (ellipse) ®, & / Action *arrow*>**GoToControl**, ®, press F6 type **[Address]** (specifies the control where you want the insertion point to move to, the Address *field*), /Save & X Macro & test your macro in your form

Conditional Formatting – to apply formatting to text when it meets a specified criteria i.e. We can program the input of "Quantity" to be displayed in red as a reminder to the data entry person that there's free shipping to those who order 5 or more of a product: Open your form in Design View, select "Quantity" Text *box* & Format>Conditional Formatting, /2nd *arrow*> Greater than or equal to, 3rd *box* type **5**, & select a Font *color*>Red, /ok. You can also format non-number fields that are associated with your "Quantity" Text box like the "Product" Text box: Go to Design View of your form: /Product Text *box*, Format>Conditional Formatting, /Condition 1 *arrow*>Expression Is & in blank box type in your expression that will extract the # "Data Type" from the "Product" Text box field of a subform, to the "Quantity" Text box & there add your criteria too, i.e. **Forms![Form Name]![Name of SubForm]![Quantity]>=5** (Note: if you don't have a Sub Form then the syntax will be: **Forms![Form Name]![Field Name]>=5**) & select same color you chose earlier for your "Quantity" Text box, /ok & /View (b), to see results…

Calendar – to create a calendar of a form for a reference & placing a command (b) on another form to /on to open your Calendar:

> 1. Create the Calendar – //Create form in Design view, On floating *Toolbox*, /the last (b) "More Controls">Calendar Control 11, & / on grid, //dark gray area (Form Properties), & /Format *tab*, & in "Caption" type **name** of your calendar, //Scroll Bars *field*> Neither, //Record Selector>No, //Navigation Button>No, //Dividing

Button (b)	Enter or Return ®	Close X

Lines>No, /Save, /Other *tab*, //MonthLength>English (Months are now full & not abbreviated), //ValueIsNull>Yes (removes today's date marker), /Save, /Form's Restore (b) /View (b) & /Save & X your calendar form

2. Create Button – to create a (b) on a form with a macro that when you /on (b) will open up your other Calendar form: Open up a form in Design View that you'd like to put a (b) that will open up your calendar. *Toolbox* turn Wizard on, then /Command Button (b) & /anywhere on your form, under "Categories" select "Form Operations" & under "Actions" select "Open Form," /Next & select "the name of your calendar form," /Next & select "Text" & type in name box **Show Calendar**, /Next & type a name for your command (b) i.e. **cmdCalendar**

3. Position Macro – to create a macro that will open your calendar to right of your screen: Create a new Macro, /1ˢᵗ Action cell, /its *arrow*>OpenForm, press F6 & /Form Name's *arrow*> the name of your calendar form. 2ⁿᵈ Action cell's /*arrow*>MoveSize, press F6 & type **4** ® /Save & X your macro. Open your form in Design View that has your calendar (b), & Right /Show Calendar (b)> Properties, /Event *tab*, /On Click *arrow*>the name of your macro you just saved, /Restore (b) for your form & size it to occupy only half of your screen & /Save /View (b), /Show Calendar (b)… (you may have to resize your form & Calendar to view both in a small 17" monitor window)

Default Date – Extra: If you wanted to view a record based upon (table or query field) a date selection the user makes from the calendar (like a project date), know that the "Value Is Null" *field* set to "No" won't work to keep calendar when opened from defaulting to Today's date: Open Calendar Form, //Dark gray area (Brings up Forms Properties), /Event *tab*, /On Load *arrow*>Event Procedure & /its Build (b), & add the following line of code **Me.Calendar.Value = Date** …(with the "Calendar" replaced by whatever name your calendar has)

Tab Pages – organizing large forms by adding tab pages, categories: Open your form that you'd like organized into categories & in *Toolbox* /Tab Control (b) & /on the form. Right /Page 1 *tab*>Properties, On Property sheet /Other *tab* & in Name *box* type in a name for your tab. From Field List add what you want in that first tab page either from your field list OR if you already have the fields on the form you can cut & paste those into the 1ˢᵗ tab page.

Add or Delete Pages – simply Right /the tabs>delete or insert.

Same Label different tab – If you add the same label with its Text box on more than one tab page you'll have to rename all their labels except the 1st one, if not you'll have to use Access's confusing default labels

Tab Order – to move your tabs around so they'll be in the order you'd like them: Right /border of Tab Control *box* (the box on your grid that holds all the tab pages)>Page Order

Tabs or Buttons – to change your tabs of your tab pages into buttons: Right /border of Tab Control box>Properties, /Format *tab*, & //Style>Buttons

Switchboard – is a form (or one big fat menu) created to help the user navigate their database easier i.e. if you have 3 forms that the user of your database will be operating with, create a switchboard or one main form for the user to have easy access to all these forms (Note: Once you created your switchboards, Access creates a Switchboard *table*; so if you want to modify a Switchboard, make the changes in its *table*: Open Switchboard Item table): Tools> Database Utilities>Switchboard Manager & select "Main Switchboard" & /Edit,

1. /New (b) & type the **Name of &Form** (placing an ampersand before any letter creates a shortcut key, and in this case Alt+F), /Command *arrow*>Open Form in Add Mode, /Form *arrow*> choose your form, /ok

2. /New (b) & type **Name of &bForm**, (shortcut key, Alt+b), /Command *arrow*> Open Form in Add Mode, /Form *arrow*>choose your form, /ok.

3. /New (b) & type **Name of &cForm**, (shortcut key, Alt+c), /Command *arrow*>Open Form in Add Mode, /Form *arrow*>choose your form, /ok

4. /New (b) & type **Close &Application**, (shortcut key, Alt+a) /Command *arrow*>Exit Application, /ok, & X switchboards & switchboard manager

Under Objects /Forms, Right /Switchboard>Rename & type **frmSwitchboard** (so you know that this switchboard is for your forms). //frmSwitchboard & view & test it

2ⁿᵈ Switchboard – You can create a 2nd switchboard aside from your main, default, if you need more. Perhaps you need another switchboard for your reports: Tools>Database Utilities> Switchboard Manager, /New & type **Reports Switchboard**, /ok. If you have 2 reports you'd like to add to this switchboard: select "Reports Switchboard" & /Edit (b),

1. /New & type the **Name of &Report**, (shortcut key, Alt+r), /Command *arrow*>Open Report, /Report *arrow*>choose your report, /ok

2. /New & type the **Name of &bReport**, (shortcut key, Alt+b), /Command *arrow*>Open Report, /Report *arrow*>choose your report, /ok

3. /New & type **Back to &Main**, (shortcut key, Alt+m), /Command *arrow*>Go to Switchb, /Switchb *arrow*>Main Switchboard, /X

Modifying – to change the label of your main switchb: Open rptSwitchboard in Design View, Right /default Label>Properties & change the Caption to **new name** ®
& you also need to rename the Label's Shadow to your "new name" too:
Notice the 1ˢᵗ option on Formatting *toolbar* (called the "Object List") that currently displays "Label 1," /its *arrow*>Label 2 & in properties find & change its Caption to **new name** ®

Picture – to insert a picture: On Formatting *toolbar* /Object List *arrow*>Picture & in Properties: /All *tab*, /in Picture *field* & /its Build (b)>browse & //your picture

Property Sheet – you can prevent this from opening by bringing up the Form's Properties: Right /dark gray area of your form>Properties, /All *tab* & scroll down & //Allow Design Changes>Design View Only

Startup – to have your main switchboard open automatically on user opening the database: Tools>Startup, & type **Name of your business**, /Application Icon's Build (b)>browse & //any icon (extensions for Icons are .ico) you'd like to add to your switchboard's title bar, /Display Form Page *arrow*>Switchboard, & uncheck "Display Database Window," /ok. To test X & reopen your database... Press F11 to open your database

Modify – to make sure when you X your database with the switchboard any hidden windows i.e. the database & adding other low security features: Tools>Startup & uncheck

Button (b)	Enter or Return ®	Close X

all 5 boxes at bottom of Startup *window*, Right /Switchboard.frm>
Design View, Bring up Form Properties, /Format *tab* & //Close
Button>No (this will disable the switchboard's Red X close (b) when you reopen
database) Test your modifications by closing & reopening your database
& note:

    1. user can't /Red X close (b) on switchboard
    2. F11 key has been disabled
    3. Right /on Switchboard>Design, disabled
    4. Tools>Startup, disabled

X the Database & this time hold SHIFT *key* & //your database to reopen,
& then you can disable the disabled items

Copy Field Macro – to copy a field in one form & paste in a field in another. Say you have a
Customer Form that contains a subform – containing several address records for
each client. A client calls to have their lawn mowed at one of their many addresses.
You want to //on any address in subform & have that address copied & pasted into
an already created street field (in Orders Table) in Orders Form using a macro: In
Design View of Customer Form, Right /Address *field*>Properties, /Event *tab*, /On
Double Click field's Build (b)>Macro Builder, Name Macro **mcrCopy to Form** &
add the following actions with their properties:

    1. GoToControl
        a. [any field but the main one you want to copy] (It's ironic that access won't go to
          the first field & later copy unless you set up 2 gotocontrols & copy on the 2nd field ?????
          beats me...)
    2. GoToControl
        a. [Addresses]
    3. RunCommand
        a. Copy
    4. OpenForm
        a. Form Name = Orders
        b. View = Form
    5. GoToRecord
        a. [Street] (Make sure you have this field in your Orders Form (based upon your Orders
          Table) that will store the addresses copied from).
    6. RunCommand
        a. Paste
    7. RunCommand
        a. SaveRecord

Reports – Reports have the exact same Design views as Forms, but different data output
views. Basically, everything is the same executing & setting up your Report as you
did above when your creating your Form (except of course you'd //Create Report using
Wizard, or if you /the New Objects Auto Form (b) and not it's arrow to the right of it>Report, you'll
get an AutoForm and not a Report)

<u>Print Preview</u> – This is the displayed report in printable format based upon the table

or query you selected when you created the report using the Wizard.

<u>Design View</u> – This is exactly the same view as in the Form's Design View (follow the steps in Form's Design view to Design, edit or manipulate your Report)

<u>Text Box</u> – Also, you can create blank Text Boxes that you can use to perform calculations based upon other Text Boxes in your Report (or Forms): To add a Text Box to perform a calculation on one *field*: On *Toolbox* (This floating toolbar is used to beautify & or help you setup to perform some calculations on those fields containing #s. If you don't see your Toolbox, on your toolbar /Toolbox (b)), /Text Box (b), then / & drag your Text Box onto your grid. Right /that box>Properties, /All *tab*, / in Control Source *field* & type **[Cost]*1.05** (as an Example, you may have a different *field* you want to increase the #s by a percentage) ®. This is a formula that was created to multiply a Cost *field* by 5%, and you could Label its new adjacent Label *box* by triple clicking on it and type in **Retail** & hit ® (Note: all fields you use in your calculations must have [square brackets] around them to identify that *field* in your form's Field List that is based upon a table)

<u>Properties</u> – The Property Sheet is used to customize the particulars of your Report (or Form) including Labels & Text Boxes. Like to change the formatting of a Text Box i.e. if its formatting is in #s, change its formatting>Currency, or if it's a Date then change its format>Long or Short Date: Right /the Text Box>Properties, /All *tab*, /Format *arrow*>Currency or Short Date etc.

<u>AutoFormat</u> – to change formats of your report: Edit>Select All (so you don't format a portion of your Report, but ALL of it) *toolbar* /AutoFormat (b)

<u>Margins</u> – if you get blank pages with some text bleeding over into it then it probably means you're exceeding the width of the page. Either change the page orientation from Portrait to Landscape or adjust the Margins: File>Page Setup and change margins or /Page *tab* & change Orientation

Hiding Duplicates – Hiding repeating info in a form. For example, if you have a customer listed in your report several times because they've ordered more than 1 product, but you only want your customer listed once with ALL of their products ordered: Right /on the Text Box that you want not repeated on your form>Properties, /All *tab*, find & //the Hide Duplicates *field*>Yes.

<u>Grouping</u> – To keep groups of info together. For example, let's say in your report you have a list of DVDs you sell & each has a field in a table that you've put into a category of Style i.e. mystery, comedy etc. You can group ALL by "Style" on your report: On *toolbar*, /Sorting & Grouping (b), & / in a blank cell under Field Expression, then /its *arrow*> Style, below /Keep Together *arrow*>Whole Group, X Sorting & Grouping. You can force each section to have its own page; starting by inserting the Report *bar* in your Design View: View>Report Header Footer, //Report Footer *bar* & in its Properties, /Format *tab*, & /Force New Page *arrow*>After Section, X Properties.

Sum Fields – To add up *fields*. For example, we want to add the *fields* in our Table: "Base Cost" & "Shipping;" & so we can get our Total Cost: 1st on *Toolbox* /Text Box (b) & name its label **Total Cost** (Bring up Properties of Label, /All *tab*, & change "Caption" *field*), then with your

| Button (b) | Enter or Return ® | Close X |

Property Sheet still open /on the Unbound Text Box (now the Properties changes from Label to the Text Box) & /in Control Source *field* & type **=([base cost]+[shipping])**

Publish to Word – to publish your Report to Word: Under object select your report & Tools>Office Links>Publish to Word

Cancel Blank Reports – creating a macro to prevent opening a report if the user enters invalid data in the prompts (prompts are parameters created in a query, & of course the form is based on that query that then prompts the user for criteria every time the user opens that report): Right /your Report> Design View this prevents the report based upon your query from prompting you), //dark gray area (Report Properties), /Event *tab*, /On "No Data's Build" (b) & select "Macro Builder," /ok & type name your macro, /ok. /1st Action cell's *arrow*> MsgBox & press F6 & type a message like "There are no records matching your criteria" ® ® /Type *arrow*>Information ® & you can type here your company's **name**. /2nd Action *arrow*>CancelEvent & /Save close macro. Open your report & when prompted invalid info to test it…

Report Chart – to insert a chart (its data based upon a query or a table) into the report. 1st you'll obviously have to create your query you'd like to see its resultant data in a chart & then do the following: Open your report in Design View & view>Header & Footer>Report Header Footer (to add a report footer if you don't have one). Insert>Chart & / on your *grid*, select queries & select the name of your query, /Next & add your fields, /Next & select a chart, /Next, /Preview Chart (b) (to see if you like what you see) & /X, /Next & select "No Fields" for both Report & Chart Fields, /Next & type a **name**, /Finish

In Columns – to shorten a single column report by converting it into 3 or more. For example, if you have a report that has a list of all your friends & their phone #'s you can put them into 3 columns on one page instead of 1 column stretching across several pages: Open your report in Design View, Add a Text Box to Detail *section*, delete its label, Right /Unbound text box> Properties, In Control Source box type **=[LastName]& ", " &[Phone]** (Note: the ampersands concatenates or joins both fields into one) *Toolbar*, /Sorting & Grouping (b) & in 1st Field Expression *cell* type **=Left([LastName],1)** ® (The "Left *function*" will group & sort 1st letter of each Last Name), copy this expression to clipboard, then //Group Header *field*>Yes, //Keep Together *field*>Whole Group & X the box Add a Text Box to the new "Group Header" *section* in *grid* & delete its label. Right /the Unbound Text Box>Properties & Paste the "Left" function in Control Source *field* (This copy of Left Function will actually ADD the 1st letter of each last name to report, remember we 1st added this function to sorting & grouping so after letter is added, it will group all last names beginning with the letter "A", then "B" etc.) File>Page Setup, /Columns *tab* & set # of columns>**3** & spacing>**.2**, uncheck "Same as Detail" & in Width type **2** & select "Down, then Across", /ok. /Save & view your report

Snapshot – to send a report electronically to anybody including those who don't have Access, (pun intended): Under object select a Report & File>Export, & name it & /Save as type *arrow*>Snapshot Format, /Export. Look in the folder you exported it to & it will be there.

Database Maintenance

Import Data – to import objects from other databases i.e. tables, forms etc., or from Excel: Right /white part of Database *window*>Import, browse to find and //your Database, then select your tables, forms etc., /ok. Excel: Right /white part>Import, /Files of Type *arrow*>Microsoft Excel, find & //your Excel Spreadsheet, /Next, check "First Row Contains Column Headings" (that is if your column labels are in row 1of your spreadsheet) /Next and follow the rest of the wizard…

Backup – In your opened Database File>Back Up Database, browse to *folder*, /Save (Note: default name has a date added)

Compact & Repair – deleted tables leave empty disk space that fragments (pigs up your hard drive space) & slows database processing time: Open the database that you've deleted any tables from & Tools>Database Utilities>Compact And Repair Database.

Password – File>Open & highlight your Database, /Open *arrow*>Open Exclusive. Tools>Security>Set Database Password & type a **password** & confirm it… /Save (Note: The only way to remove password is you have to Open the Database "Exclusively" again and enter password & then you can: Tools>Security>Unset Database Password)

Object Dependency – before deleting an object check to see what's dependent upon it i.e. Right /any *table*>Object Dependencies, /ok

Performance – a way for Access to analyze your database & suggest performance improvements: Tools>Analyze>Performance, /All Object Types *tab*, /Select All (b), /ok

XML Data – XML (Extensible Markup Language) is a go between program of software that is incompatible because of differences in versions or programming. If you have one program that you want data pulled from and put into another incompatible program you can export it first as XML and then import that XML into your other program.
Schemas (XSD) – are sets of rules that defines how XML can be used i.e. defining "Data Types," and hold info about the structure of the data, and are saved with the extension XSD (Extensible Schema Data) and not XML.
XSL – Can be used to transform data in an XML file, or used to apply formatting with the XSLT (Extensible Stylesheet Language Transformer).
Import – Right /white space of Database>Import, //an XML file, /ok, /ok.
Export – Right /a table>Export, /Save As type *arrow*>XML, /Export, /More Options, /Schema *tab* & uncheck "Include primary key and index information," (optional to uncheck) /Browse (b) & select a *folder*, /ok, /ok.
Export to HTML – Right /any Access Report>Export, /File type *arrow*>XML,

Button (b)	Enter or Return ®	Close X

/Export, /More Options, /Presentations *tab* & check "Export Presentation," /ok.

Split – to split a database so that you can put your tables on the backend server & the other Objects: Forms, Reports etc. (frontend) are located on the user's machines.
1. <u>Pro</u> – The admin has only one copy of the database to manage & protect. Doesn't have to visit each users machine to keep them updated.
2. <u>Con</u> – Database must be set so there won't be bottle necking & lock the database up if a large # of users hit database at same time, & users need read/write access to Tables so thorough security measures must be set.
Open your database & Tools>Database Utilities>Database Splitter, /Split, (<u>b</u>ack <u>e</u>nd Default Name is same name but has added '_be.mdb' to name), /ok (Split may take time depending on size of database & speed of computer).
   1. (Note: Tables with arrows to left of them mean they are linked to backend)
   2. (Note: Create your Switchboards AFTER you Split because the switchboard table has to reside on frontend & not with the rest of the tables on the backend)

Security Front & Backends – to protect both backend & frontend after a database has been split (*see* Split Database). Security terms & definitions…
1. <u>Encryption Decryption</u> – Compacts your database & renders it unreadable by a word processor or utility program (good for storage or electronic transfer)
2. <u>Hide Objects</u> – to hide database's object, but easy for anybody to unhide
3. <u>Startup</u> – to specify what user sees when database is opened
4. <u>Password</u> – to set an encrypted password for ONLY opening the database (Note: this can't be used if you ever plan to replicate the database)
5. <u>VBA Code</u> – to keep unauthorized users from editing, cutting, pasting, copying, exporting, or deleting your VBA code.
6. <u>Data Access Page</u> – to set Internet Explorer's settings to prevent unauthorized access to data access page
<u>Frontend Security</u> – When you install access you're automatically made a member of a group named "admins" with a user account named "admin." By default, you also have an empty password & Personal Identifier. Until you activate the logon procedure, the Admin user account remains hidden: Open your Frontend database (database you used to split), Tools>Security>User-Level Security Wizard (Note: the wizard creates an unsecured backup of the database, because if you forget your password you're TOAST! And you will have to recreate your database over again), /Next, /Next & let them all be checked so ALL are secured, /Next & select each Group & read about it (The Admin Group is included by default) & check boxes accordingly, /Next & select accordingly, /Next & select "Add New User" & in User Name type **Person's Name** & a password for them (Note: password is case Sensitive & be sure to write passwords down!), /Add this User to the List (b), /Next & add your name to the "Admin" *group*, then add the other users to your choice of Users *groups*, /Next, /Finish & read the report… (Note: the report has user names & their passwords too! Saved as a .snp or Snapshot file. Store it in a save place) X the Snapshot file & /ok to accept encryption & X Access. On Desktop find your database's shortcut & //it (Note: database is secured, but your backend database database_be.mdb is an unsecured copy of your database.mdb) & log on as the admin. File>X (don't exit out of Access or you'll be

| Mouse Click / | To > | Task Pane <u>TP</u> |

exiting out as admin too & if you do, you won't be able to do Backend Security)…

Backend Security – File>open database_be.mdb & Tools>Security>User-Level Security Wizard, make sure "Modify…" is selected (If not that means you've go to //Shortcut to database.mdb (frontend) on desktop & log on as admin & FILE>CLOSE & FILE>OPEN the database_be.mdb (backend) or these next steps won't work), /Next & make sure all Objects are selected, /Next & check: New Data Users, Read-Only Users & Update Users, /Next, /Next, /Next, /Finish File>X & /Yes to save as Snapshot file & X Snapshot. Tools>Security>User and Group Permissions, select Radio option "Groups" & select "a group" & assign or remove permissions, /ok

Distribute Database – to backup & then distribute Frontend (to users) & Backend (to server) databases after they've have security measures applied to them from steps above. Note these following steps are for PC networking without a server, but same concepts are easier applied to a server:

1. Copy database_be.mdb (including its shortcut) & Secured.mdw (mdw file stores info about the members of the group) to a shared directory *folder*
2. On User's PCs: Open *any* folder & Tools>Map Network Drive & pick a letter i.e. Z as the drive letter of the shared directory folder.
3. On Administrator's PC: On Desktop //database.mdb's *shortcut* (frontend) & log on as Administrator & Tools>Database Utilities>Linked Table Manager (to re-link this master copy to the mapped drive Z:) & check all tables & check "Always Prompt for New Location," /ok & browse to mapped drive "Z" & //database_be.mdb (backend)
    i. Copy the re-linked App.mdb AND App.mdb's *shortcut* into the shared directory & then from the shared directory copy the App.mdb AND App.mdb's *shortcut* onto each user's PC
    ii. Remap the database.mdb *shortcut's* Target *address* 1st to User's own computer's Access Database folder MSACCESS.EXE, 2nd to the own user's desktop storing a copy of the frontend database, 3rd to the Secured.mdw file in same shared directory drive. For example, if we created a Z drive on a User's computer the shortcut's…
        1. Target to the database.mdb file would be as follows (In Windows XP of course): **"C:\Program Files\Microsoft Office\Office10\MSACCESS. EXE" "C:\Doccuments And Settings\User Name\Desktop\App. mdb" /WRKGRP "Z:\Secured.mdw"** AND the
        2. Start In **Z:**

Password – to add a password to database so when emailed, if intercepted, no worries. Also, this the 1st line of security defense and if they break through that you'll have workgroups, switchboards & permissions: Open Access 1st & log on as admin & then file>X the database & then file>open & highlight yourdatabase.mdb (you must log on as admin first & close the database without exiting the Access program so Access can retain admin privileges & by-the-way is a warning to when you're an Admin ALWAYS exit Access completely or somebody else can log on as you), /Open *arrow*>Open Exclusive &Tools>Security>Set Database Password & type in password

Button (b)	Enter or Return ®	Close X

<u>Remove</u> – File>Open, highlight database.mdb, /Open *arrow*>Exclusive & Tools>
Security>Unset Database PasswordProtect VBA Code Protect VBA Code

Protect VBA Code – to prevent unauthorized users from deleting, editing, copying your VBA code:
Select any form in Database & on *toolbar* /Code (b) & Tools>L4Base Properties,
/Protection *tab* & /Lock & for password type password, /ok.

Encryption – Encryption compacts the database & makes it great for storing or sending your database
electronically (it's also good as a 2nd level of security aside from having a password): With only
Access opened (not databases): Tools>Security> Encode Decode Database select
database.mdb, /ok, select database.mdb again & /Save, /Yes.
<u>Decrypt</u> – to Decrypt follow same procedure as above…

.MDE Extension – turning .mdb files into .mde files to protect your database from
someone copying the application & the supporting codes. .mde files prevent users
from:
1. Viewing, modifying or creating <u>forms</u> in Design View
2. Viewing, modifying or creating <u>reports</u> in Design View
3. Viewing, modifying or creating <u>modules</u> in Design View
4. Add, delete or change references to database or object libraries
5. Changing source code
6. Import or export forms, reports or code modules
Qualifying factors in order to save your .mdb as .mde file:
    1. Must remove replication if any to the database
    2. Have complete Admin privileges
Access Program (no databases open): Tools>Database Utilities>Make MDE File &
select database.mdb, /Made MDE (b), /Save

Convert 2000>2002-2003 – Tools>Database Utilities>Convert Database>Access 2002-
2003 select database.mdb, /Convert & name it, /Save, /ok

Link to Excel – to link Access to Excel: Right /in white database area>Link Tables, /type
arrow>Microsoft Excel, //Excel Workbook.xls, & select a sheet & /Next, check 1st
row contains column headings, /Next & type a name, /Finish, /ok

Refresh Links – to update your table to backend source: Right /any table>Linked Table
Manager, /Select All, /ok

Replicate – the concept here being able to create a copy of database, make changes on the road, come back
& ANY changes made on either the database's will update both! (Note: the replica of the original can
only have records updated, not designs): Open database.mdb & Tools>Replication>Create
Replica, /Yes, /Yes & name it, /ok, /ok (Note: yellow *icons*, & you're not in the Replica, but
back in the Design Master). X the Design Master, copy the Replica of the Master to your
laptop & make all the changes you want with the records. When you're back at the
office you can synchronize your replica with original & ANY changes made on

either side of the Master or Replica will update in the other i.e. Open the Replica database.mdb, Tools>Replication>Synchronize Now, browse to find the Master database.mdb & //it, /ok, /ok

Data Access Page – Data Access Pages or DAPs are web pages based on your tables (like your Forms) that you can publish to the web and update your tables through the web or network. Limitations: To deploy, the user must have Microsoft Office 2003 license & its Web Component (which comes with Office) installed on computer. For outside users to view your DAPs, must have Internet Explorer 5.5 or higher, although the viewer doesn't need Access on their computer, they do need MS Office Web Component installed on their computer, and the Web Component has to be equal to or higher than the software the DAP was created with for best results. Access 2003 DAPs won't install on the older OS's: Windows 95, 98 or ME. To create a web page: Under Objects, /Pages & //Create Page Data Access Page in Design, in Field List, find the name of a table you'd like to base your Web page on & /its plus + sign to expand it & drag the *fields* from the list to the page grid, /ok. /Save & name your web page (This saves a web page & creates a shortcut *icon* under "Objects" in Pages).

Dropdown List: Scenario: let's say you have an Employee ID # field in one table & the names of your employees in another table. To display both the EmpID field & their names from separate tables in a combo box, first create a query that has EmpID field & another that concatenates (combines) the first & last name field. To create a Dropdown List that will list concatenate names
1. In Field List expand a table to reveal the *field* EmpID
2. On Toolbox /Dropdown List (b) & from Field List / & drag EmpID onto Access Page (this creates the EmpID dropdown field, but without any functionality, you'll have to add that next…)
3. Right /*field* you just added to your page>Element Properties, /Data *tab* & /Control Source *arrow*>EmpID, /List Row Source *arrow*>your concatenate query, /List Display Field>field from the query that concatenates EmpInfo & /List Bound Field>field from the query EmpID (this binds the EmpID from the table to the EmpID in the concatenated query) & Width>Auto (this will do an auto fit to the largest line of text), /View (b)…

Dropdown List 2: Scenario 2: let's save you have in your customer table a field that has your customers listed as seasonal clients A, W, S, Su for Autumn, Winter, Spring & Summer. To display those codes in a Dropdown List…
1. *On Toolbox* /Drop-down list (b) & /in Access Page: & select "I will type in the values I want," /Next (Note: most # of columns allowed is 2) in 1st row *cell* type **A** (for Autumn), 2nd row *cell* **W** (Winter), 3rd row *cell* **S** (Spring), 4th row *cell* **Su** (Summer), /Next & for label type **Seasonal**, /Finish
2. Right /Seasonal Text box>Element Properties, /Control Source *arrow*>the name of the field in you the table containing your seasonal codes, in Default Value *field* type **Su**, /Width *field's arrow*>Auto (Note: List Row, List Display & List Bound Field Properties are blank)…

Group Records – to group records it's easier to start by using the Create DAP using wizard: //Create DAP using Wiz, select your fields you want to use, /Next & //a field you want to group your records by (Note: that field will be added in the Preview window, and to remove it, in the Preview window, //that field again)

Button (b)	Enter or Return ®	Close X

Browser – to view Access Pages in Browser to preview: File>Web Page Preview

PivotTable – creating PivotTables in DAPs: //Create Data Access Page in Design View, On Toolbox /PivotTable (b) & /on grid, TP, expand folders & drag & drop fields to Row, Column & Filter Fields in a fashion that you'd like to see the data appear in your table & /Save.

Remove Fields – Right /a *field*>Remove Field.

Rename Column Headers – Right /a column *header*>Command & Options, /Captions *tab* & change to change caption or to change formatting, /Format *tab*, /Number *arrow*>Currency, X

Column Totals – to create Totals and Grand Totals for your columns: On Pivot Toolbar, /Auto Calc (b)>Sum

Pivot Chart – In Design View on Toolbox, /Office Chart (b) & /below your PivotTable, then Right /that chart>Field List & select "Data from the following web page item" & select the name of your PivotTable (Default Name is: PivotTable0).

Change Size – to change size of your chart: Right /perimeter of your Chart> Object Properties enter your #s in the Height & Width *fields*

Themes – to add a preformatted design to your web page: Format>Theme & select one, /ok.

Hide Records – to prevent user from viewing all records already entered in database, except those the user enters in themselves: Edit>Select Page & in Property Sheet, /Data tab & /Data Entry arrow>True

F11 – will bring Database *window* up front if hidden behind other *windows* or if it's completely hidden, and not locked by Admin for security

Ctrl+F11 – Toggles between custom menu & built-in menu

Ctrl+G – Brings up Immediate window

Ctrl+Break – Pause the application

Alt+11 – Opens Visual Basic

| Mouse Click / | To > | Task Pane TP |

Publisher

Publication From Design – a specified group of colors applied to the presentation like to text & boxes: Open Publisher TP: /Publications For Print (expands & has sub-categories) & when you've narrowed it down, look into the Preview *window* on the right & / or //one to a final (Note: if this is your first time using Publisher a Personal Information *window* will open up where you can add your business's email, website, phone etc. that will be automatically applied to every Publisher template you use from here on out. To edit you personal info later: Edit>Personal Information)

Blank Publication – to create a publication from scratch without using Publisher's default templates: TP: /Blank Publications (Note: if you don't see your TP, File>New) & in Preview *window* /Full Page.

> Ruler Guides – are green guides you add to help align objects on your page: Arrange>Ruler Guides>Add Vertical or Horizontal (Note: To move guides, / & drag. To remove guides, / & drag it off the page. You can add more than one Horizontal or Vertical guide, but they will layer on top of each other, or another way to add more than one guide Ctrl+/ & drag a guide)

> Add Text Box – boxes you put on your page & enter text into: Left of TP: is Objects *toolbar* & on it /Text Box (b) & / & drag on your page to draw the box, when finished you can type in your text (Note: if you can't see your text, zoom in by pressing F9 *key* & press it again to zoom out! 2nd Note: you can Ctrl+/ & drag a Text Box already on your page to create a duplicate of it)

> Add Picture – add one of your own pictures saved on your computer: Objects *toolbar*, /Picture Frame (b)>Picture from File, & / & drag a frame onto your blank page, then a *window* opens up for you to browse your computer for photos, find one & //it

Page Editing – Press F5 *key* to quickly go to a page #

> Insert & Delete Pages – one you have at least one page, look at bottom of your *window* &: Right /that little page numbered *tab*>Insert Page or Delete

> Insert Text File – After you've added all your Text Boxes, you can type in your text, or if you have a Word Document, insert it: select a Text Box on your page you want to insert text from a saved Word Doc & Insert>Text File find your Doc & //it (Note: if the text you inserted is too large to fit in box, then you can /Yes to have Publisher automatically choose other Text Boxes to flow your text into, or /No to create them yourself & manually connect the text, *see Connecting Text Boxes*. 2nd Note: If the text you entered is too much for the size of your Text Box, you'll see an overflow "A…" symbol – telling you there's more text than meets the eye in the box, & only displays itself when that Text Box is selected)

> Resizing Objects – to shrink or stretch a Text Box or other object, select it &: /one of its white *handles*, & drag it in or out to stretch it, or Right /it>Format Object, /Sizing *tab* & enter the size of your dimensions manually (Note: if you change the height of your object & suddenly the width changes to, then here you'll want to uncheck "Lock aspect ratio," to keep the other dimension from matching your changes).

> Moving Objects – to move a Text Box or other object: Simply hover your mouse over its border till you see a four-way arrow, then / & drag it (Note: once selected you can also use your arrow *keys* to move it minutely).

> Move Pages – to move a page: Bottom of window, /a numbered *tab* like 3 & drag it to

| Button (b) | Enter or Return ® | Close X |

right of say Page 7.

Connecting Text Boxes – when there's an overflow of text & you want the rest of the article to continue on a later page>a 2nd Text Box: /in the Text Box that displays the overflow "…A" *symbol*, & on Connect Text Boxes *toolbar* /Link (b), now go to the page that contains your empty Text Box you want to overflow the text into & /in it & watch the text fill over from your 1st Text Box (Note: immediately after you / & the text is added, a green *arrow* is at the top of the Box, /on it & it will take you to its linked, previous Text Box. & it works vice-versa).

Add Captions – once you've linked the Text Boxes you can add captions that will point the reader to the correct page that the article they're reading continues on. For example, say you linked 2 Text Boxes: Right /the 1st Text Box>Format Text Box, /Text Box *tab* & check "Continued on page," /ok (Note: you might have to Zoom in 100% to see the caption). Next Right /the 2nd Text Box>Format Text Box, /Text Box *tab* & check "Continued from page," /ok

Text Box Into Columns – dividing Text Boxes into columns, For example: Right /a Text Box> Format Text Box, /Text Box *tab*, /Columns (b) & in "Number" type **2** & for "Spacing" **.25**, /ok, /ok

Add Middle Line – to add a separating line between columns: Right /Text Box again> Format Text Box, /Colors & Lines *tab*, /Center Vertical Line (b), /Color *arrow*>Black, /Style *arrow*>1pt, /ok

Format Text Boxes – added fill colors or borders, for example: Right /Text Box>Format Text Box, /Colors & Lines *tab*, in "Fill" *section* /Color *arrow*>More Colors & select any color, /ok & in "Line" *section* /Color *arrow*>More Colors & select any color, /ok, /Weight>any pt. to make border thicker or thinner, /ok.

Master Page – a page where you can include text or objects on every page in your publication: View>Master Page (or Ctrl+M) & Insert>Page Numbers, /Position *arrow*>any & /Alignment>to any & uncheck "Show…", /ok (Note: find your inserted page # symbol at top or bottom of your Master Page & /before it & type **Page**, that way you'll know in normal view what the #'s mean with the *word* Page next to it.

Headers & Footers – to add headers & or footers: View>Header & Footer (takes you to header) & type in a **header** (Note: on Header Footer *toolbar* /Switch (b) to go to Footer where you can type in your **footer** text), on Header Footer *toolbar* /Close (b) when done (Note: after exiting out of Header & Footer view & you decide you don't want those viewed on page 1 of your publication then: View>Ignore Master Page).

Research Words – use MS Publisher's Research TP to look up words in an online dictionary, encyclopedia etc. For example: Right /any word>Look Up, TP: scroll down & /Thesaurus, Right /any word>Insert

Find & Replace Text – Edit>Replace TP: in "Find what" type a **word**, press Tab *key* &

type a **word** you want it replaced with, /Find Next to find it & then /Replace

Spell Check – Right /any word that has a red squiggly line underneath it>the correct word, or on *toolbar* /Spell Check & follow the prompts.

Format Text – To change the format of your text to bold, italic & color: 1st Select your text & Format>Font & choose your formats here & /ok when you're finished.
Format Painter – Used to copy multiple format styles from one text to another: Find some text that has some formatting (like bold, red, size 24 etc.) you'd like to copy & apply it to some plain text, then / in it so your cursor is flashing in the middle of it & on *toolbar* /Format Painter (b), then find some text & drag your brush over it. (Note: Your Format Painter will only paint once & disappear, unless you //the brush, and it won't stop painting until you / once on the brush again or hit ESC *key*)

Schemes – applying a specific set of colors or fonts to your publication for consistency i.e. color or font schemes: Format>Color Schemes (or Font Schemes) & in TP: select a scheme i.e.

Insert Symbols – Insert>Symbol, /Special Characters tab & select © /Insert (b) & X, or Insert>Symbol, /Symbols tab, /Font arrow>Wingdings, select a picture symbol, /Insert (b) & X.

Indent Paragraphs – /in any Text Box & up on the Horizontal Ruler, on the left side are 3 small Indent Markers that can help adjust your paragraph's indentations:
First Line Indent – top triangle; when you / & drag it right, it indents 1st line of paragraph.
Hanging Indent – middle triangle; when you / & drag it right, it indents all but 1st line of your paragraph.
Left Indent – bottom rectangle; when you / & drag it right, it indents the whole paragraph
(Note: there's also a Right Indent *marker* on far-right of Horizontal Ruler)

Spacing – For single, double or customized line spacing, even paragraph spacing: /in the paragraph you want to change its line or paragraph spacing, on Formatting *toolbar*, /Line Spacing (b), /Indents & Spacing *tab*, & in "Line Spacing" *section* set either you paragraph spacing either "before" or "after" it, or line spacing, /ok (Shortcuts: Ctrl+1, Ctrl+2, Ctrl+5 for 1.5 line spacing).

Line & Paragraph Breaks – keeping paragraphs or lines together, or from breaking apart when part of it is at the bottom or top of a page: Select your paragraph you want kept with the paragraph below it & on Formatting *toolbar*, /Line Spacing (b), /Line & Paragraph Breaks *tab* & check "Keep with next" (again, this keeps paragraph selected with next paragraph, or from being separated. 2nd Note: the Widow Orphan is checked when you have a single word that is by itself at the top of another column, the orphan, & it looks funny by itself, check this box & some of its friends, not a lot, will join him & not leave him alone), /ok.

Button (b)	Enter or Return ®	Close X

Paragraph Styles – you can have several formats under one name, which when name is applied, so are all its formats. You can create your own or use Publisher's defaults: Formatting *toolbar* /Style *arrow*>Headings 1, 2 or 3 . To create your own then: Select some text you want your style applied to, & make the changes to it first, like change its Font>Arial & its Size>18, & /**bold** /Align Center (b), then on Formatting *toolbar* /in Style *box* (Not its *arrow*)& type in the **name** of your new style & ® (Whatever you have selected & enter a name in the Style *box*, that's what formats will be sucked into & named as the new style)

Format Picture – like to add a border to your picture: Right /your *picture*>Format Picture, /Colors & Lines *tab*, in "Line" *section* /Color *arrow*>Black, /Weight>any pt, /ok, /off picture...

> <u>Crop</u> – to cut in a portion of your picture: On Picture *toolbar*, /Crop (b) & /on one of your Picture's border handles & drag it into the picture as far as you like ... /Crop (b) again to turn it off.

> <u>Text Wrap</u> – you can have text wrap around a picture to look a bit more professional: Right /your *picture*>Format Picture, /Layout *tab* & select a wrapping feature, /ok then if you haven't already, drag your picture into you text & if your picture is small enough the text will wrap around it according to your selection.

WordArt – To add more visual pizzazz to a word on your document: Select your word & on Object *toolbar* /WordArt (b) & select a format, /ok, change its size & /ok.

Design Gallery – is a collection of pre-designed objects i.e. Mastheads, Table of Contents, Logos, & Pull Quotes (that take a quote & makes it stand out!) & more that you can use instead of creating one from scratch, & you can also modify the objects too, for example: Objects *toolbar* /Design Gallery Object (b), & select its sub-category "Logos," in Preview *window* /on your choice (Note: once added you can delete the text on the Logo & replace it with your Company's Name)

> <u>Save Custom Logo</u> – after opening & customizing a the logo to fit your company's desires, you can save it to use later: Select entire logo, Insert>Add Selection to Design Gallery, type in Object Name *box* a **name** & in Category *box* type **Logos**, /ok. To find custom Logo to use in another publication: On Object *toolbar* /Design Gallery Object (b) & /My Objects *tab*, /your logo to add to your page!

Design Checker – this checks for design errors i.e. a Text Box or picture partially cut off: Tools>Design Checker, <u>TP</u>: will display any problems it find for you to Right /on>Go to this Item or Right /on>Fix...

Graphics Manager – used to list all pictures in your publication in <u>TP</u>, along with options to manage them: Tools>Graphics Manager, Right /any listing in <u>TP</u>: for *menu* of choices.

Create Email Newsletters – you can send the publication as an attachment in an email or as an actual background email for marketing that can include web links to your website and more!: File>Send E-Mail>either as an "attachment" or "Send This Page as Message" (NOTE! When you "Send This Page as Message" the user will get your email as a background stationary that will look really nice and functional with any hyperlinks you've added, but WARNING! But make sure NONE of your Text Boxes that contain text are touching other Text Boxes or other objects, because if so,

| Mouse Click / | To > | Task Pane <u>TP</u> |

then your text will convert to an UGLY graphic image & the best way to test before sending it is: File>Send E-Mail>Email Preview, because what you see is what they're going to get! 2nd Note: to create Hyperlinks for you marketing Newsletter, *see* Create Webpage's *Hyperlinks*).

Create Webpage – to create a webpage(s) for your company's website, use one of Publisher's many easy to create templates: TP: /Web Sites & Email, then select a sub-category "Web Site" & select its sub-category "Easy Web Site Builder" then in Preview *window* /on your choice, & a *window* will pop-up for you to check what you want to do with your website & /ok (Note: pages will all be linked together, what you have to do is make sure you type in or add objects in to replace the default text). You can then preview & test your web page publication by: File>Web Page Preview & test some links... Note: the Home Page's blue Title Bar says "Home," and to change it: In TP: /Page Content & scroll down & /Rename page *link* & replace Home with a new **name**, /ok, File>Web Page Preview to test!

Hyperlinks – Select some text you'd like as a hyperlink in your Web page &

> Insert>Hyperlink (or Right /it>Hyperlink), & in largest window browse & //a file you want linked to it (Note: any files you link to on your computer you'll have to load them up on your Internet Service Provider's Server too)

> Email – to create a link for web page viewers to /on that will open up their email with your email address in their To: field: Select the text you want as an email *link* & Right /it>Hyperlink & in Link to *section* /Email Address, & type **youremail@somename.com** (Note: mailto: will be added to email address, but leave it as its part of the program), in Subject *box* type the name of a general subject i.e. **Tech Support**, or **Please Tell Me More About Doughnuts**, /ok.

> External Links – to link your text or an object to another's website: Select your text or object & Right /it>Hyperlink & in Link to *section* /Existing File or Web Page, in Address type **www.disney.com**, /ok.

Save Publication As Web Publication – to convert a print publication>a web publications: File>Convert to Web Publication & follow prompts (Note: Be sure to /Save as a different name so you still have your original, unconverted web publication)

> Publish>Server – talk to your Internet Service Provider for the address folder and help in submitting your web page or site to their Server.

Template – once you create a basic structure of a publication, you can save it as a template where you can use it over & over again as a basis for all your new publications. For example, say I was publishing four quarterly newsletters and my basic design for the newsletter on same pages will ALWAYS be the same. First create your newsletter with only those basics in mind, then: File>Save As, /Save as type *arrow*>Publisher Template & type a **name** in File name *box*, /Save. Now whenever you're starting a new quarterly newsletter i.e. for 2nd or 3rd quarter, you already have the basics save, so open your template & use it: File>New TP: /Templates (if templates isn't there then X out of Publisher & reopen it), make changes to it for 2nd quarter & save it as **Quarter 2 2004**.

Shortcuts

Toolbars – If you every need a specific *toolbar* Right /any available *toolbar*>find one or

Button (b)	Enter or Return ®	Close X

View>Toolbars

| Mouse Click / | To > | Task Pane TP |

Project

Project's Schedule Date – to either schedule the project to start on a certain date or schedule a project from a finish date (from finish date means that *any* time added or taken away after project has been built, will push the start date of the project to start earlier or later, but *must* finish on finish date): Project>Project Information, /Schedule from *arrow*>Project Start or Finish Date & then /Start or Finish *arrow*>a date

Gantt Chart – When opening Project, 1st view is called Gantt Chart, consisting of 2 views: Left is *table* & right is Gantt Chart (But ironic both views as one are still called the Gantt Chart)

> Zoom – to view all tasks in chart: View>Zoom, /Entire Project, /ok (Zooming crunches the timescale depending upon the over all length of the project i.e. your project's default timescale views tasks day-by-day, when you zoom, it could crunch it to every other day, or every other 3rd day, etc.)

> Timescale – is the time bar displayed directly over the chart of the Gantt Chart *view*, to change the time on how you view your tasks by day or hour: //Timeline

> View Bar – a display bar to help user navigate around different views in Project. To show View Bar: View>View Bar (Note: you can also Right / on View Bar>display common Views without having to scroll in to other views in View Bar).

Project Calendar – by default Project is based on a Standard Calendar (M-F, 8-5pm with 1hr lunch 12-1pm). Making changes to the standard template will apply to all new projects, or you can create a calendar based on standard where you can make changes that won't apply to all new projects. Also, if there's a conflict between resource calendars & the Project's, resource *always* takes precedence: Tools>Change Working Time, /New & /Make Copy of *arrow*>Standard (8-5 Workday with 1hr lunch) or Night Shift or 24 hour & type in name of your calendar i.e. **Doughnuts**, /ok...

> Change Default Times – to change the "default" working times of your "Doughnut" Project Calendar, say from a standard 8hr work day shift to 10 (Note: "Resource" or "Task" *Calendars* will always take precedence over your Project's Calendar, because hey! You can't force a worker to work or a task to complete on time): /Options (b)

> Holidays – to schedule days off on project calendar: /For *arrow*>Doughnuts *calendar*, then /on a day & over to the right select "Nonworking time."

> Working Hours – to customize a certain day's working hours from the standard 9-5pm: / on a day you want to change hour from 8-5 to **9-5**, & over to the right, replace the current hours with your desired hours. For mass selection, in that calendar /on the *headers* M (for Monday) & it will select *all* Mondays

> Assign Project A Calendar – To assign your project a calendar (after you created it): Project>Project Information & /Calendar *arrow*>Doughnuts *calendar*.

Tasks – in Gantt Chart's table, enter each task you'd like to have worked on in the, project in successive order. If your project is going to have phases, be sure to enter each phase as a Task, and its corresponding subtasks below. For example...

> Creating Outlines – are high-level tasks that can keep track of the total # of days of all its low-level tasks or subtasks, i.e.: Type in all 3 tasks, starting with our phase task 1st "Electrical": Task 3 type **Electrical**, Task 4, **Air Conditioning** & Task 5, **Heating**. Select both tasks you want as subtasks to the Electrical phase, i.e.

| Button (b) | Enter or Return ® | Close X |

Air Conditioning & Heating & on *toolbar* /Indent (b) (Note: both now look like low-level tasks. Also note that Electrical will count the # of days of the longest task, but if you want Electrical to keep track of the total sum of both tasks then you'll have to link your 2 subtasks together, *see Relationships*)…

Show/Hide Outline – once all the subtasks are indented an outline is created. Note the – sign left of milestone task: / on – sign to collapse subtasks & - changes> + ready to show again its subtasks when you / on it, or on *toolbar*, /Show (b)>hide or view levels of your outline…

WBS Codes – (Work Breakdown Structure Codes) when checked all tasks will be assigned a # that is representative of the Outline structure i.e. All Milestones will be given a whole # (2, 3, 4) & each subtask will be assigned a decimal of that whole # (2.1, 2.2): Tools>Options, /View *tab* & check "Show Outline Number," /ok

Milestone – Tasks with **0** duration (represented by a Black Diamond in Chart), & is used to mark particular events i.e. **Start** or **End** of the project, or for unknowns.

Rearranging Task Order – if after you entered your tasks & want to move them around i.e. say task 5 you want moved up above Task 2: /the row *header's* #, 5 (this selects entire Task 5), /5 again & drag it above Task 2.

Duration – to set the amount of time each task is required to be completed: The column, just right of Task Name, Called "Duration" (Note: if you don't see it then either scroll over, or drag the thin "Split Bar" separating the Gant Table from Gantt Chart,>right till column is visible), then type in the duration of all subtasks: i.e. **1m** (1-minute), **1h** (1-hour), **1d** (1-day), **1wk** (1-week), **1mo** (1-month), (Note: all milestones will only show the duration for the *longest* subtask, and to get a total duration for *all* subtasks the subtasks *must* be linked in a relationship, *see Relationships*)

Project Summary – a task name that summarizes your project's goal: Tools>Options, /View *tab* & in "Outline options" check "Show Project Summary Task," /ok. Select Task 0 & type **name** of your project

Recurring – a task that occurs over & over again i.e. a doughnut meeting: Select the task that you want to insert your recurring doughnut meeting before it & Insert> Recurring Task & type **Doughnut Meeting**, Duration type **2h**, */arrow*>Every Other & check Monday, /Start *arrow*>any date, /End by *arrow*>date, /Calendar *arrow*>the Project's *calendar*, /ok

Go To – to quickly go to, & view one Task's *bar* in the Gantt Chart: Select a task in Gantt's *table* & on *toolbar* /Go To Selected Task (b)

Insert & Delete – Right /Task Row *header* #>New or Delete i.e. I want to insert the task "Carpet" between the task # 5 "paint" & #6 "Move furniture in." Right /Paint's row *header*, #6>New Task & type **Carpet** ®

Linking – to give flow to tasks in a project, links (or relationships) are created between all tasks in successive order. So after the links are created, for example, when one task finishes the next one will start & so on. But 1st you must link all tasks together: Select the tasks in order of completion by first selecting the 1st task & then holding the Ctrl *key* & selecting their successors until all task are highlighted (WARNING! When using the Ctrl key you have to highlight each task in order. In other words, if you select task 1 & Ctrl+/ task 8 & then task 2 the relationship will be… when task 1 is completed start task 8 & then task 2. If you made a mistake in the order of highlighting tasks, / off in a blank area to deselect & start over), & then on *toolbar* /Link (b) (Note: The Gantt Chart shows blue bars, and when one task is done, a blue arrow points to the next task to start, & this default is called the Finish-Start relationship – when this task finishes, the next one can start, *see Relationships*)

Break Links – Select task(s) to be broken using Ctrl *key* & on *toolbar* /Unlink

Relationships – when a task is linked to another task it creates a default Finish-to-Start relationship so when this task if finished the next one can start. There are 4 types of relationships:

1. Start to Start
2. Finish-Finish
3. Finish-Start (Project's default)
4. Start-Finish

To help decide what type of relationships to use, fill in the blanks of the following sentence with one of the 4 types i.e. Start-Start:

The predecessor must ____ before this task can ____.

To change a relationship: //a task, /Predecessor *tab* & change its default Finish-to-Start by selecting it 1st & then /its *arrow*>any relationship, /ok (or //the thin blue lines between tasks in the Chart)

Lag & Lead Time – //on any task, /Predecessors *tab* & in Lag *field* type in a negative # of days for "Lead" or positive # days for "Lag"…

    Lag – A delay between 2 tasks; that adds waiting time

        Slack Time – is the amount of time a task can slip before affecting other tasks & or a project's finish date. To view slackers: View>More Views, //Detail Gantt, View>Zoom & select "Entire Project" (Note: little green lines are slack; hover other them for pop-up notes)

    Lead – Starting a task a day or more before its predecessor finishes; also a – 30% entered in Lag field would mean the task would start after predecessor is completed 70%

Notes – To insert notes: Right /any task>Task Notes & type in your **notes**, /ok. Hover your mouse over Note *icon* in Indicator *column* to view its pop-up *tag*

Constraints – will limit a Project's flexibility by altering its schedule. So it should only be used when absolutely necessary and even then it's best used only on the last Task of your project to prevent original project's end date from delaying without a warning to the user: //any task you'd like to place a constraint on, /Advance *tab* & /Constraint Type *arrow*>to a constraint for the task, then /Constraint Date *arrow*>a date you want it constrained to, /ok (Note: hover over tag in indicator column to get a pop-up of the type of constraint placed upon)

Deadline – is a better way to identify a deadline without project altering the schedule & preventing scheduling flexibility: //any Task, /Advance *tab* & /Deadline *arrow*>any date, /ok (The deadline can be seen in gantt chart as a green down pointing *arrow*. The green simply is a visual marker and does nothing more. You can also hover over the green *arrow* with your mouse for a pop-up reminder)

Critical – is a task that must finish on time or it will bump the project's end date out. To view all critical tasks that: In Gantt Chart on *toolbar* /Gantt Chart Wizard (b), /Next, Select "Critical Path,"/Finish, /Format It, /Exit

Updating – to keep track & update a task's progress: View>More Views, //Task Sheet, then View>Table>Tracking, Select a Task's %Comp. *field* & enter a # in the % complete ® (Note: after % complete is entered, MS Project calculates the Actual & Remaining Work & Costs for resources assigned to the task. If you want to do this manually

Button (b)	Enter or Return ®	Close X

without MS Project's help then: Tools>Options, /Calculation *tab* & uncheck "Updating task status updates resource status"). Now enter Actual Duration: in the Act. Dur. *field* enter any # of days, and or enter the Actual Cost, Work etc.® (Note: don't enter the "Actuals" before the current date or MS Project will calculate funny results)

Splitting – splitting a task is usually done when a task has started, but then encounters a delay & hence the rest of the task is split to finish at a designated later date: In the Gantt Chart hover your mouse over the Task's blue *bar* & Right /it>Split Task, then slowly move your pointer over the same task bar & find a date to break the task & / (Note: the task is now split, but only delays the 2nd half of the split task out 1-day, if the delay is more simply / & drag the 2nd half of the task out as many days delay as desired)

Combine – to combine a split task back into a whole one: Hover over the 2nd half of the task until you see a 4-way arrow (it's a bit tricky) & then / & drag 2nd half back to 1st half.

Rescheduling – like Task Split, if a task is incomplete & will complete at a later date: Select a task marked partially completed & Tools>Tracking>Update Project & select "Reschedule uncompleted...," & /its *arrow*>any date i.e. 8/16/09 (the remainder of the task will always start the day after the set date so this one will start on 8/17/09) & select "Selected Task," /ok

Slipping – to view all task that have slipped: On *toolbar* /Filter *arrow* from "All Tasks">Slipping Tasks. To remove Slipping Filter change Filter *arrow* back to "All Tasks"

Resources – Materials and or Work you use to complete a task. To create the resource list: View>Resource Sheet, type in a resource **name** & in...

1. **Type** *column* – 2 types of resources: work (i.e. laborers) & material (wood, shingles etc.).
2. **Material Label** – If the Resource Name is Shingles, & the "Type" you selected is "Material" you can give it a Material *label* that the Shingles come in i.e. Bundles. So when you assign this resource to a task you assign it in Bundles i.e. 25 Bundles
3. **Group** – this field can be used to group resources i.e. for each resource, assign it a group of **Internal** or **External**, & then on *toolbar* /Filter *arrow* (currently displaying "All Resources">Group & type in **External** & only those resources will be displayed. To ungroup, /Filter *arrow*>All Resources.
4. **Max Units** – is for # of people. 100% equals 1 person or laborer.
5. **Std. Rate** – is rate for laborers entered hourly, monthly or yearly i.e. 14/hr, 2000/wk, 5000/mo & 55000/y
6. **Ovt. Rate** – Over Time
7. **Cost/Use** – is a one time fee.
8. **Accrue At** – defines when costs of that resource are to be paid; either Prorated (as task is completed), Start (start of a task) or Finish (when task is finished).
9. **Base Calendar** – tells what calendar is being used or to use.

Calendar – All work resources entered in the "Resource Sheet" as "Work" Type resource, Project will automatically create a Resource Calendar for it: After creating the resource, //on resource, /Working Time *tab*, & customize the working hours, or set the days off.

Availability – to set when the Resource is available: /General *tab* & /Available From *arrow*>any date & then /Available To *arrow*>any date (Note: if you had 100% Max Units, eventually it will read 0% because this resource isn't 100 % available *all the time* that's why it's a good idea to insert a side note with it to remind you why it's not 100%), /Notes

| Mouse Click / | To > | Task Pane TP |

tab & type in a **note** about this resources availability, /ok (the Note icon is displayed in the left most column called the Indicator column, & when you hover over it with your mouse, the note pops-up)

<u>Assigning To Tasks</u> – To assign a resource to a task: 1ˢᵗ select a task, & Window>Split (to remove: Window>Remove Split) At the bottom, in Split Window, under "Resource Name" / in blank *field* & then /its *arrow*>any Resource, /ok (Note: resource isn't assigned until you /ok). By default 100% (or 1 resource) is assigned i.e. After we assigned 1 Electrician, we can change our minds to assign more by changing 100: to **200** (for 2 Electricians), or for 1 part-timer enter **50** (50%=4hrs out of an 8hr day) & /ok (Note: only assign as many Electricians as you have in your Resource Sheet under Max Units. Also note: once assigned Gantt Chart will display the Resource's name adjacent to it blue Task *bar*)...

<u>Remove</u> – remove resource from a task: in Split Window /on Resource & hit Delete *key*, /ok

<u>Effort Driven</u> – depending upon what Task Type in Split Window...

1. <u>Fixed Units</u> (default setting) – Assigning additional resources will shorten the Resource's *Work & Task's* duration
2. <u>Fixed Duration</u> – Assigning additional won't decrease Task's duration, but instead shortens the Resource's *Work & Units*, or
3. <u>Fixed Work</u> – is *always* checked as Effort Driven. Assigning additional will divide the *Work* between all resources but the total Work for the Task is fixed; i.e. the only time you'll notice a difference is when changing the duration won't affect the Work hrs (unlike changed the Duration on Fixed Duration), but the Unit's percentage (Note Fixed Work is always Effort Driven)

...you've selected along with "Effort Driven" being checked for each Task, will determine what is cut in half & shared between 2 or more work resources assigned to the task. The "operative" word for each Task Type is *Fixed*, meaning, if you assign more than one resource to a task, what ever is *Fixed*, won't be shared or cut in half to compensate for the additional help...

- <u>Fixed Units *example*</u>: Let's say then that we have a task, Ditch Digging that requires 8hrs to complete. Effort Driven is checked. You assign 1 laborer to it & it's still an 8hr task, but when you assign a 2ⁿᵈ laborer to it, the duration of the task is cut in half so each laborer is only required to work 4hrs. Then you assign a 3ʳᵈ laborer to it. Then the 3 laborers works 2hrs & 40 minutes each. Never will the Units, the percentage of laborers, change because the task type is Fixed Units. Note: if Effort driven isn't checked, then all 3 laborers work 8hrs each, totaling 24hrs on ditch digging.
- <u>Fixed Duration *example*</u>: Effort Driven is checked. The task is 16hrs long. You assign 1 laborer to it, nothing. When you assign a 2ⁿᵈ laborer, the duration of the task remains 16hrs to complete, but both laborer's Units are cut from 100% to 50%, meaning each laborer is only required to work part-time on the task. Because the task is 2-days long, then each laborer will show up and work only 4hrs, totaling an 8hr day. Then come back the 2ⁿᵈ day to finish up the 16hr duration. Never will the Duration, the amount of days of a task shorten because the task type is Fixed Duration.
- <u>Fixed Work *example*</u>: Effort Driven is checked. The task is 16hrs long. You assign 1 laborer to it, nothing. When you assign a 2ⁿᵈ laborer, the duration of the task is cut in half to 1day to complete, and the 2 laborer are required to work 8hrs each. Never will the Work, the amount of hours of a task shorten because the task type is Fixed Work.

<u>Not Effort Driven</u> – for some project managers having the duration, work or units cut in half when adding additional resources isn't practical and so most turn off Effort Driven for each task. The only thing to keep in mind is: when you assign more than 1 resource to a task and you want to customize the total duration or resource's units, and or work without effort driven on, and you're not getting the correct results, you'll want to check

| Button (b) | Enter or Return ® | Close X |

the Task Type and change it accordingly.

Overallocated – if any resource is working more than the standard 8hrs a day then the resource is overallocated or stressed. One way to see if your resource is stressed is: View>Resource Usage. Any resource in red is stressed (Note: You can also contour your resources here by changing their individual work hours – more flexibility and less problems if you do your contouring when you create your project and not contour in the middle of it) & to go to the exact stressed dates: View>Toolbars>Resource Management, on that *toolbar* /Go To Next Overallocation (b). You can also Right /anywhere in the yellow *grid*> Overallocation, or "Remaining Availability" to show those fields in comparison to the grid's default Work *field*

Solutions – by default MS Project will overallocate any resource (put it in red) if that resource is working more than 8hrs a day. Following are some solutions to manage those overallocated resources & keep them out of the red...

Overtime – assigning overtime: In Gantt Chart, Window>Split, /on task & Right /anywhere in bottom window>Resource Work & in Ovt Work *field* enter # of overtime hrs for each resource, /ok

Leveling – is a process Project uses of delaying or splitting tasks to avoid conflict & as a result can delay the Project's finish date: In Resource Usage *view*, select the overallocated resource & Tools>Level Resources, /Level Now, select "Selected Resources," /ok. To see what tasks were bumped around: View>More Views, //Leveling Gantt (In chart *green* bars are pre-leveled & *blue* are post-leveled)

Clear – to clear leveling: Tools>Level Resources, /Clear Leveling...

Cost Table View – Project has many views & also has many tables per view. The default Table view for Gantt Chart is "Entry." You can view the "Cost" of each task by changes the Table's view (not the view itself i.e. Gant Chart, on it's table): View>Table Entry>Cost (Note: if you every feel lost in Project, regarding the views, ask yourself 2 questions: (1) What View am I in? (2) What Table am I in?)

Baseline – is a base that doesn't change & is used by project managers to compare to "Actuals" and how far off the base they are like on project's duration, task's start & finish times, costs and more. Saving a baseline takes a snapshot of those fields at that time & saves them for later comparison. Project XP can save up to 10 Baselines: Tools>Tracking>Save Baseline, /ok. To clear: Tools>Tracking>Clear Baseline, select your baseline from *menu*, /ok.

Project's Stats – to view overall of your project's statistics such as current costs, baseline costs, start, finish & actuals: Project>Project Info, /Statistics (b)

Project Summary Report – View>Reports, //Overview, //Project Summary

Importing – you can import from Excel & Access, but the import is limited to only items in projects as Tasks, Resources & Assignments...

Excel – In project File>Open, & /Files of Type *arrow*>Excel, //your Excel file, /Next, select "New Map," /Next, & select 1 of 3 ways of importing into your Project, /Next & select the 1 of 3 types of data your importing (the only views in Project that Project will allow Excel to import into is Tasks, Resources or Assignments),

Mouse Click /	To >	Task Pane TP

/Next & /Source worksheet name *arrow*>a worksheet in your workbook containing your data. Left *column* reveals name fields in your worksheet to be imported & in Right *column* /in corresponding *field* & /its *arrow*>a field name you wish it imported into Project (this requires that you know the field names in each Project's views i.e. if I created a workbook for Tasks that I want imported, it doesn't matter really what I named the title of my Tasks column in Excel like 'TNames,' so long as I map it to the correct field in Project, named "Name"), /Next, /Save Map (Save the map if you are going to do this a lot, so you don't have to remap field from your Excel book>their field counterparts in Project every time), /Finish.

Access – follow same steps and concepts used in Importing Excel

Export – you can export certain data from Project into Excel from its default Templates, or you can export snapshots of views into Word or as a web Page…

Excel – File>Save as, /File Type *arrow*>Excel, /Save, /Next & select "Selected Data Option," /Next & select "Use Existing Map" (only if you have one previously saved, or would like to use one of MS Project's templates like "Cost Data by Task"), /Next, select "Cost Data by Task" & you can /Finish.

Picture – take a snapshot of a view in Project & paste it into MS Word for a variety of reasons, but one could be to email off to those who want to view parts of your project but don't have Project installed on their computers: In Gantt Chart on *toolbar* /Camera (b) & select "For Printer" (black & white so doesn't use up expensive color ink), & then open MS Word & /Paste

Web Page – to a copy of project in a universal readable format, a web page: File>Save as Web Page & type name of page & /Save, /Next, select "Use Existing Map" & /Next, select "Export to HTML…" & /Next, /Finish

Tracking Gantt – will show the baseline and compare it to the Task's "Actuals" in the chart: View>Tracking Gantt (Note: if a baseline has been saved the chart will display it as a black bar for each task).

Progress Line – in the Gantt Chart you can display a red line, that when straight means all tasks are on target and marks the current date, but if any part of the red progress line bends back on any task, it means that task is behind schedule & if it bends ahead or forward, then task is ahead of schedule). Right /in Gantt Chart>Progress Lines & check "Always Display Current Progress Line" & select "At Current Date," /ok

Tracking Toolbar – mainly used to mark of percentage of task completed: Right /any *toolbar*> Tracking. Select a task & /a percentage (b) on Tracking *toolbar* to mark its state of completion.

Variance Table – This table has 2 columns that compare the current Start & Finish *fields* of each task to its Baseline, & displays those differences in the Start & Finish Variance *columns* i.e. all negative #s in Start or Finish Var *column* means that the tasks are finishing early (-2 means finished 2 days early, and like wise all positive #s): View>Table>Variance

Interim Plan – only saves or takes a snap shot of start and finish dates of each task at time saved, & up to

Button (b)	Enter or Return ®	Close X

10 interims can be saved: Tools>Tracking>Save Baseline & select "Save Interim," /ok
Custom Table to View Interims – View>Tables>More Tables & select Baseline, /Copy (to make a copy of the Baseline view to edit) & for Name type **Interim Dates** & check "Show in menu" (this will display 'Interim Dates' Table in the Table *menu*). Delete any fields (Rows) you don't want to see in your table. Then /In a blank *row* & /its *arrow*>Start 1 (This is Interim Plan 1) ® then go to Start 1's Title *cell* & type in its name as **Interim Start 1** ® Repeat for Finish 1 & each additional saved Interim Plan i.e. Start 2, Start 3 etc. too…, /ok, /Apply

Custom Fields – creating a custom field & inserting into any view as a custom column to help manage your data in project…

Text – This field is a generic one to create because anything can be entered into this field including text & #s for whatever you need an extra field for: Tools>Customize>Fields, /Type *arrow*>Text (this type is for a field that will allow you to type in any text), /Rename & type a **name** for your custom field, /ok, /ok. Right /any Column *header*>Insert Column & /Field Name *arrow*>the name of your field, /ok.

Remove Columns – to hide a column like Task Name, Right /its Column *header*>Hide

Flag – This field is a yes or no field which again is used for anything you can think of that is a yes or no situation for a task i.e. if certain tasks need to pass an inspection, this custom field can display a happy green face for yes or a frowning red face for no: Tools>Customize>Fields, /Type *arrow*>Flag (To check any custom field's values like this Yes No Flag, /Value List (b), /in Value list *cell* & /its *arrow* to note 'Yes''No' Values, /Cancel), /Rename (b) & type in a **name** for your field (Note: if you don't rename it, it may not be able to proceed through the next steps), /ok, /Graphical Indicator (b)…

1. /Test for *arrow*>equals & under value type **Yes**, /Image cell's *arrow*>a HAPPY FACE.
2. Repeat step one but this value type will be **No** with FROWN FACE…, /ok, /ok (Note: if you don't repeat this step for "NO" then the cell will remain blank, even if you select "No" from the Flag field list later)

Right /any column header>Insert *column* & /Field name *arrow*>Flag 1 or the name of your flag & test its fields in the column i.e. /in them first & then selecting… then /off somewhere when done to see a HAPPY FACE or not!

Hyperlinks – linking task to a document or spreadsheet: Right /any task>Hyperlink & browse to find a document & //it. (Note: the link to / on will only display itself in the Indicator *column*, & if you don't have that column, then Right /any Column *header*>Insert Column, /Field Name *arrow*>Indicators, /ok to insert Indicator *column*)

Custom Reports – View>Reports, //Custom, /New, /ok, for Name *field* enter a **name** for your report, /Table *arrow*>any table that interest you to base the report on, /ok, /Preview…

Headers & Footers – Then /Page Setup, /Header *tab* & under its Center *tab* delete & or enter info that will be displayed on all pages of the report in the header's center. /General *arrow*>Project Title & /Add (to insert Title of Project), & or /General *arrow*>Project Current Date & /Add, & or /Page Fields *arrow*>

Mouse Click /	To >	Task Pane TP

%Complete & /Add & after the interested code type **Complete** (to label what the # inserted represents, which is again the %Complete), & or /Footer *tab* & under its Left *tab* & /Insert Picture (b) & browse & //any picture you'd like as part of your report & /Print Preview…

Print Range – some of MS Project's reports will allow you to customize the date spread to be printed: /Close, to close out of the Print Preview & back to Custom Report selection *window* & select "Task Usage" & /Preview… (Note: many pages, but we can narrow the date to be printed…) /Print (b) & change the date to print from i.e. 10/6/09 to 11/9/09, /Preview…

Templates – you can create a basic project with tasks & outlines that can be saved as a template to copy & base future projects off of it: File>Save as, /File Type *arrow*>Template & type name of template, /Save & check what types you don't want saved into your template, /Save & File>X. File>New & in TP, /On my computer *link* & //your template. Now when you save this it won't overwrite your template(.mpt) but Save as a copy of it (.mpp)

Custom Views – to create your own specialized views. There are 2 types, single view & combo:

Single – View>More Views, /New & select "Single View," /ok & type a **name** for your view, /Screen *arrow*>a desired screen, /Table *arrow*>to a closely corresponding table of desired view, /Group *arrow*>No Group, /Filter> All Tasks, /ok, /Apply

Combo View – this view will display two views in a horizontal window split in Project: View>More Views, /New & select "Combo," /ok & for Name type a **name**, /Top *arrow*>a view, /Bottom *arrow*>another desired view, /ok, /Apply

Organizer – is used to copy almost anything custom made, like Views, Tables, Calendars, Reports, Forms, Fields etc. into another project or onto the Global Template so your customs can be displayed in all *new* projects. Also, this is the place to delete them from your project as well: Tools>Organizer, Left *pane* contains Global Template & in Right your current opened Project. /the appropriate *tab* i.e. Calendars & in Right *pane* select a custom calendar you want *always* in all new projects created from here on out & /Copy (b) (it copies that selected field over to the Global Template). To share only between 2 projects & not put custom on Global Template: You must open up the 2 projects & in the Organizer's Left *pane*, at the bottom, /its *arrow* from Global>your 2nd opened project's name & then you can now copy between the 2.

Share Resources – if you have resources that many other projects will be using, the best thing to do is to create & save a Project with only the resources listed in the Resource Sheet and nothing else & name it **Resource Pool**, then after: open up a project that will be using resources from the "Resource Pool" & Tools>Resource Sharing>Share Resources & select "Use Resources," & make sure From *field* displays "Resource Pool," /ok (this will then make a copy of all the resources form the "Resource Pool" into your project's Resource Sheet).

Overallocation – when sharing resources from same pool, that pool will keep track of all resources, in that you can find out when you assign a resource if that resource is overallocated because some other project is using that resource at the same time. For example, after assigning a resource to a task in your project: View>Resource Usage & look for red resources to

Button (b)	Enter or Return ®	Close X

see if overallocated & if so there's no current way of getting MS Project to displaying how many other projects are using that resource & specifically what times, so you'll have to do the investigation yourself.

Master Project – is a project that oversees subprojects. Any changes made in subprojects will be updated in Master & any changes in the master will be updated in the subprojects as well, for example let's first start with a blank Project, Save it as **Master,** Tools>Options, /View *tab* & check "Show project summary task," /ok & note your first Task is Task 0, properly titled **Master,** then /in Task 1 and: Insert>Project, & browse to find your project, then //it (Note: the title of the inserted subproject is displayed as Task 1, with a + sign that will expand to reveal subproject's tasks). /below Task 1 (in a blank Task field 2) & insert your 2nd subproject & repeat steps as necessary. (Also, you can link your subprojects in relationship i.e. Finish-to-Start to continue one after another in your master, just like you did with your tasks)

Microsoft Project Server – after your IT person has set up the server for MS Project, then the Project Manager is able to do the next couple of steps to manage his project on the server & also how others can access that server. Note: Client Access License (CAL) is needed for each person who wants to view your project on the server.

Publishing Project To Server –

1. open your project you want on the server & Collaborate>Collaboration Options: /Collaboration using *arrow*>Microsoft Project Server. In URL type (your IT dude ought to provide this to you, something like...) **http://server/projectserver**, then /Test Connection (b)..., /ok. Under "Identification" select "Window user account" (This allows access to Project Center without having to log onto the Project Server separately, but logs on using your Window user account), /ok

2. Publish – Collaborate>Publish>Project Plan, /ok (to save after published), /ok (to publish Plan). If prompted "make trusted site," /yes, /ok (now snapshot of your Project is on server)

3. View Published – To check & see if project was published we can use your opened Project as a window to the Server: Collaborate>Project Center (Project Center is Home page. If you use User Names at your office to log on, you'd enter them at this point), /the name of your project's *link* (to display published project plan's task), then in upper-right corner. When finished confirming, /Click Here To Close This View *link* (Note: Deleting Info from Server you will need your administrator to help you out)

Assign Resources – Next to assign resources to your tasks & publish it to server so later when the resources log on they can accept or reject assignments:

1. Select a task in your project & if you haven't done so already assign resources to it. With Task 2 still selected: Collaborate>Publish>New & Changed Assignments, /ok (to save Project after published), /ok & select 'Selected Items' & uncheck 'Notify...' (if not using email), /ok (to publish), /ok

Review Resources – this is how your resources will log on to view their assignments:

1. The resource opens up the Internet & goes to the web address designated by the IT dude i.e. http://server/projectserver & log in (again the IT person can give them log in names & passwords).

2. Under 'Tasks' /the new task *link*, /on the assigned *task* (Note: Indicator Column for task has a *sparkling* Task *icon*; it will display only once when its first viewed), /Go

Mouse Click /	To >	Task Pane TP

To Task (b) to view task assigned.

Request Progress – to request progress reports from your resources on a specific task:

1. In Project: select a task you want a progress report on & Collaborate>Request Project Info, /Request Progress Info for *arrow*>Selected Items, /From *arrow*>& select a date, /To *arrow*>ending date (Note: Indicator column will eventually display an 'envelope with a clock & a ? mark' indicating that your project is waiting for an update report on the task), /ok…

Actual Work – once the request has been made, now it's the resources turn to enter in their actual work on their end:

1. Resource goes to website & logs in, (Note: task indicator *column* has a ? mark; saying that Project Manager has requested progress info)
2. /Timesheet view *link*, then expand 'View Options,' /Date Range *arrow*>select the date, /To *arrow*>end date, /Set Dates & then Collapse 'View Options.'
3. In left pane scroll>Actual Work *field* & type actual hours work & hit ®
4. Select the *task* & /Update Selected Rows (to send update for approval from Project Manager), /ok (Note: indicator has changed from ? mark to a Sheet with a ? mark: saying its been sent but not updated in project plan)

Accept Updates – now the project manager is back in his project & can check and accept any updates: Collaborate>Update Project Progress. /in Accept? *cell* to left of the *task* for the 1ˢᵗ resource, & /its *arrow*>Accept. Repeat steps for rest of *resources*. Upper-right *corner*, /Update, /ok (saves project to server), /ok, /ok. Then in upper-right *corner*, /Click Here To Close This View *link*…/Save.

Shortcuts

Change Table View – In Gantt Chart, on Gantt Table, there's a blank Column *header* above your Tasks # 0 or 1, Right /it>change your Table's *view*!

Windows XP

Starting Computer – turn all devices on like monitor 1ˢᵗ

> <u>Boot</u> – When a computer is turned on & is loading OS i.e. Windows XP & besides a regular boot, there are 2 other types…
>
> > <u>Warm</u>: When you need to restart or reboot your computer because your computer has frozen. Simply, find on your keyboard the keys Ctrl, Alt & Delete *keys* & press & hold all 3 (Ctrl+Alt+Delete) at once, two times & your computer will reboot.
> >
> > <u>Cold</u>: When your computer has frozen up so badly that you can't perfom a Warm Boot, but must press & hold the on the box's (Computer) Power (b) for more than 5-seconds and the computer will shutdown. Wait for it least 30 seconds before turning the computer back on or you could damage computer by turning computer on & off too quickly.
>
> <u>End Application</u> – Sometimes you can end a program that freezes up without having to reboot your computer, of course you'll loose whatever you've created in your program, unless you've previously saved it before it froze, but then again you'll lose it anyway with it frozen forever: On your keyboard, find the keys Ctrl, Alt & Delete & press & hold all 3 at once (Ctrl+Alt+Delete) just one time. Then click once on the Program that will say "Not Responding" & click the /End Task (b) & wait to see if it will end it in about a minute. If it doesn't end it then reboot the computer (Note: Follow the steps above if your computer freezes up, don't automatically pull the plug or push your power (b), as at that moment or perhaps over time that will damage your computer)

Desktop – The first screen you see with all of your icons i.e. My Computer, Recycle Bin are sitting on your "Desktop"

Mouse – Has 3 buttons: Left, Middle & Right

> <u>Left</u> – /once to select an object or icon, //twice to open a *folder* or execute a program
> <u>Middle</u> – Roller is used to scroll up and down in documents or websites
> <u>Right</u> – Right /once to view shortcut menu or properties of a *folder* or program

Menus – 3 types of menus

> <u>Start</u> – Start (b) has a menu
> <u>Right Mouse (b)</u> – when / typically brings up a shortcut *menu*
> <u>Window</u> – Open a *folder* or application and it opens a window with a *menu* at the top

Windows – A folder or application when // on will open a window for you to view what's inside.

Window Properties – The main features of a window includes the following…

> <u>Title Bar</u> – The blue *bar* located at top of window with the Title of you window
>
> > <u>Minimize</u> – The first of 3 (b)s located on Title Bar, far right: / it to minimize (compress) your window down to the bottom of your screen on the Task Bar, in the shape of a rectangle (b), & / that (b) to maximize window to full view.

Restore – is 2nd (b) of 3 on Title Bar: /on it to Restore your window to a smaller size (less viewing area); but when same 2nd (b) is / again it will maximize window to full view of your screen or monitor

Close – Last (b) on Title bar looks like an X: /it to Close the window

Manual Sizing – Hover your pointer over any 4 borders of your window to see a two-way arrow, then /& drag out or in to manually resize your window

Menu – Below Title Bar, and is used to manipulate features within the window

Toolbar – Below Menu, and holds most commonly used (b)s to edit a window

Scrollbars – Only appear when there's more info in a window that can be seen: To view the info you use the scroll bars located to the right and bottom of each window.

Taskbar – The thin blue *bar* with the "Start" (b) at the bottom of your screen is called Taskbar

Buttons – For every window that is opened you will see a corresponding (b) for it on your Taskbar

Moving – To Move your Taskbar from bottom to top of your screen: /on blank area of Taskbar & drag it all the way to the top of your screen (it will be invisible until you let go of mouse (b) at top of your screen. Note: you may not be able to move it if its locked. To unlock it Right /a blank area of your Taskbar>Lock the Taskbar or likewise you can lock it to keep it from moving by following same steps to check "Lock the Taskbar")

Clock – found on right-side of Taskbar. Make sure your clock is correct as you'll find out later that most other programs base their time on it i.e. when you create a document the time of its creating is stamped on it (see Properties). To set your clock: //the clock & make your changes & /ok when finished.

Properties – Right /any folder, icon or file on your Desktop>Properties to find summary info of : For example, //My Computer and Right /C: drive>Properties and see how much space is available left for you to use on your hard drive.

Control Panel – Controls the software and hardware on your computer like…

Mouse – To adjust / speed of mouse: Start (b)>Control Panel & /Printers and Other Hardware & /Mouse

Keyboard – Adjust typing speed: Start (b)>Control Panel & /Printers and Other Hardware & /Keyboard

Display – To change Desktop wallpaper or screen saver: /Start (b)>Control Panel & /Appearance and Themes, /Display

User Accounts – To add a password to your logon, or you can add or remove other users to your computer with a login name & password; that way the user can use the same programs installed on your computer, but won't be able to see your personal data stored on your log in…

Add Password – to add a password to your account: Start (b)>Control Panel & /User Accounts, /Change Account & /on your Log in name or icon, & /Create Password & follow instructions…

Add or Delete User – if you have one computer in your family & 3 brothers & sisters who want to use the computer, but you don't want them to have access to your data, then create a user account where they can't see your data, nor you view theirs without their password: Start (b)>Control Panel & /User Accounts, /Create a new

| Button (b) | Enter or Return ® | Close X |

account, type in first users account name **Joe**, /Next & read the details of each option, but you may want to select "Limited" (Note: this prevents other users from adding accounts or deleting them, but also may prevent them from installing some programs), /Create Account… Next to you restart your computer or Log Off, Joe will be able to log on to his own account.

Microsoft Interactive Training – you can have Microsoft help you learn Windows XP interactively: /Start (b)>All Programs>Accessories>Microsoft Interactive Training>Microsoft Interactive Training, /ok & expand a *folder* (clicks its plus + sign) & find a file of interest & //it.

Help & Support – questions about Windows XP or need to troubleshoot: /Start (b)>Help and Support & search for your answer either by typing in keywords or scrolling through the index.

Search – if you can't find a program or file you know is on your computer, then let the computer help you find it: /Start>Search, <u>TP</u>: under "What do you want to search for?" /on 1 of 4 green arrow (b)s i.e. /All files and folders (b) & you type in part or all of a **file name** in top *box*, or if you don't remember the file name you can type a **word or phrase** you think is inside the document or file & then /Search (b)… (any files to be found will show up in your Search window, //your file to open it).

Windows Explorer – To see & manage all of your folders and files in one view: Right /Start (b)> Explorer – Left *pane* is a list of all *folders*, Right *pane* shows all the subfolders and files of the *folder* you have selected in the Left *pane*.

Create Folder – Right in a blank area on your Desktop>New>Folder, & immediately type in **name** of your folder & press ® to have it accept the name.

<u>Rename</u> – Right /any *folder*>Rename and immediately type in a new **name** & press ® when finished

<u>Move</u> – To move a *folder* you can / & drag it to your desired place, or you can Right /it>Cut and open another *folder*, then Right /inside a blank space>Paste

Create & Save A Document – to open up WordPad to type a letter & saving it after typed: /Start (b)>All Programs>Accessories>WordPad & type your letter, when finished, File> *Save*…Note: if this is the 1st time your saving a document if will default to *Save As* that will ask you two questions:

1. Where do you want to save your document? /Save in *arrow*>a desired place like your Desktop
2. What's your document name? In File Name *field* type the **name** of your file, /Save (b) when finished.

After you saved your document for the 1st time you can File>Save and it won't ask you any more what to do.

<u>Save As</u> – If after having saved the document your 1st time, & you'd like to create a copy of your document: File>Save As and simply type a new **name** in File Name *field* &

Mouse Click /	To >	Task Pane <u>TP</u>

/Save (b), now you have the original document and a copy of it with a different name.

Recycle Bin – Basically, it's the Garbage Can found on your Desktop. When you delete anything on your computer it will go to the Can and sit there until you decide to empty it: To empty your Recycle Bin Right /it & then left / on Empty Recycle Bin in *menu*

Program Shortcuts – To create a shortcut to an original *folder*, application or document: Right /anything you want to create a shortcut to i.e. a folder>Send To>Desktop (create shortcut)
> <u>Modify</u> – To change appearance of your shortcut: Right /the shortcut>Properties, /Customize *tab*, /Change Icon (b) & either select a default one or /Browse & search your computer for a picture & //it, /ok, /ok…

Start Menu – The Start Menu is nothing more than a bunch of shortcuts & if you created a shortcut (*see Shortcuts*) you can add it to your Start menu: / & drag your shortcut onto the start menu & wait for it to expand then drag it to a spot & let go of the mouse. To Remove: Right /a shortcut>Delete

Calculator – Windows XP has a calculator you can use: Start (b)>All Programs>Accessories> Calculator… (Note: you either the mouse to / the #'s or use your key pad on your keyboard. 2nd Note: when you have the total you can Ctrl+C (shortcut for Copy), & open your WordPad & Ctrl+V (shortcut for Paste))

Personal Computers or PC – PC's are used on or beside a desk for one user. There are 3 types of PC's (Note: *IBM* machine or clone i.e. HP, Compaq, Toshiba, Gateway, Dell, Sony and more… & *Macintosh* i.e. iMac, are currently the two major manufacturers in the industry):
> 1. <u>Microcomputers or Desktop</u> – Is the largest & hence the most powerful of PC's & was meant to stay at a desk, not lugged around.
> 2. <u>Notebook or Laptop</u> – Portable computers the size of a notebook, or can fit on a person's lap.
> 3. <u>Handhelds</u> – mini computers that fit into your hand. Operate on batteries and aren't that powerful, but some Doctor's office use them to wirelessly connect to their bigger Desktop computers, to look up and or enter a patient's record (with a pen, called a "Stylus," on the touch sensitive screen) on the spot, as they bounce from room to room.
>> a. <u>PDA</u> – Personal Digital Assistants are palm-sized computers, as personal organizers
>> b. <u>Palm Computers</u> – Look like PDA's but can have external keyboard & mouse attached.

Hardware – computer, monitor, printer, anything you are able to physically touch.
> <u>Internal Device</u> – something that can be installed inside your computer.

Button (b)	Enter or Return ®	Close X

<u>External Device</u> – something that can be plugged in or connected on outside of your Computer

Software – programs stored on the computer & is accessible only when it's turned on, there are two types:

1. <u>OS or Operating System</u> – is the go between you & your PC, helps start your computer when you push "On" (b) i.e. Windows XP is an OS, like it's predecessors: Windows 2000, 98 or 95. The OS is like a playground where all the application programs can come out and play…

2. <u>Applications</u> – Programs created to do a specific job in its own window i.e. the game "Solitaire," or business applications such as Excel, Word, Access, PowerPoint and Outlook (these programs are referred to as Office applications or programs, but people confuse this with the Windows OS. Office XP & Window XP are completely separate i.e. Windows XP starts your computer & sets it up so you open and run an office program like Excel XP, or to play movies, music or games i.e. Heroes III, *see Application Programs*)

Input Device – Sending info into computer i.e. keyboard, mouse or scanner.

1. <u>Scanner</u>: Used to scan documents on to computer.
2. <u>Mouse</u>: A rolling device that has 2 buttons & a tail like a mouse that connects to the back of your box. Buttons on mouse used to open or execute programs
   - <u>Click</u>: Press left mouse button once; used to select item on screen.
   - <u>Double-Click</u>: Quickly press left mouse button twice; used to execute a program or open a file.
   - <u>Right-Click</u>: Press right mouse button once; used to display a shortcut menu for that item your pointer is on.
   - <u>Left Drag</u>: Press & hold left mouse button while moving mouse; used to move folder or other items.
   - <u>Right Drag</u>: Press & hold right mouse button while moving mouse; used to move or copy folder or items (after you release right mouse a short cut menu will show prompting you to copy or move item).
   - <u>Middle Wheel</u>: Roll the wheel: used to scroll through pages of a document or internet.

Output Device – Computer showing you info i.e. monitor, printer or speakers.

Storage Systems – Devices used to store your work permanently when you close out of your work and shutdown your computer.

<u>Floppy Drive</u> – A device that uses floppy disks to record data & is assigned the letters A or B by computer, but typically A, or A Drive.

<u>Floppy Disks</u>: 3.5" disk you can save your work to & use on other computers. Most floppy disks are HD or High Density disks that store 1.44 MB (About 250 pages of a document). Don't press hard on the flat surface of floppies or store them in the sun, or near magnets (i.e. speakers)

<u>Hard Drive</u> – Located in the box (Computer) & the current, average Hard Drive stores about 160 Gigabytes (Each DVD can hold up to 4.7 GB), and runs faster than a

floppy. Assigned a letter by the computer C or called C Drive.

CD-Writers – Compact Disk Writer, Drive or Burner that records info to your CD-ROM, CD-R or CD-RW disks

> CD-R: This type of CD can only record data one time only, but be used or read many times (Note: can store 700 MB of music, about 80 minutes worth).

> CD-RW: Can record (or write) info up to 1000 times & read many times.

DVD Writers – Digital Video Disk drive or burner that records data to your DVD-ROM

> DVD-R: This type of DVD can only record data one time only, but be used or read many times (Stores 4.7 Gigabytes, 1 Gig = 1024 MB. Note: Some DVD's can have double layers that can store almost twice as much data on same side i.e. over 8 GB).

> DVD-RW: Can record (or write) data up to 1000 times & read many times.

Zip Drives – Zip drives look like floppy drives, but are slightly bigger & store more i.e. 100 MB to 1 GB, & are faster than floppies but not as fast as a Hard Drive.

Jaz Drives – Like a Zip Drive but faster & stores up to 2 Gig or GB.

Drive D, E or F – Depending on how many CD-Writers or Zip drives you have installed in your box (Computer), with a letter assigned by your computer to each one.

Printers – different types & are based upon the quality measured in DPI's or Dots Per Inch; or resolution of your printers ability to print smoother text & pictures, the higher the better.

Dot Matrix: are almost outdated or not used as much, and have 9 or more pins to pound the ink stained ribbon on to the paper & the resolution is limited to 180 dpi.

Ink Jet: Has tiny nozzles in the head that inject ink onto paper that dries instantly & averages 300-1200 dpi. Prints an average 3ppm (Pages Per Minute)

Bubble Jet: Pushed in out of its nozzles by expanding bubbles and have a better resolution for pictures even though same in dpi as Ink Jet 300-1200.

Laser: Uses laser light to write images around a photosensitive drum & the sensitized areas around the drum attract toner powder to print on paper, 300-1200 dpi.

Applications Or Programs – software designed to perform a specific purpose (Note: even though this list only contains business programs, games are applications too).

Word Processing – To create documents.

> *1. WordPefect*: Made by Corel Corporation.

> *2. Word*: by Microsoft

Spreadsheets – Do mathematical calculations and store client info as a database.

> *1. Excel*: Microsoft

> *2. Lotus 1-2-3*: IBM Corporation

> *3. Quattro Pro*: Corel

Presentations – Create a slide show.

Button (b)	Enter or Return ®	Close X

1. PowerPoint: Microsoft

2. Corel Presentations: Corel

Database Management – A collection of data like clients and vendors

1. Access: Microsoft

2. Paradox: Corel

Graphics – Creates or manipulate pictures

1. CorelDraw: Corel

2. Illustrator: Adobe Corporation

3. Photoshop: Adobe

4. Visio: Microsoft

5. Freehand: Macromedia, Inc.

6. Dreamweaver: Macromedia, it also creates web pages.

Multimedia – to create & or view animation for the web

1. Flash: Macromedia

2. Director: Macromedia

3. Shockwave: AtomShockwave Corp. used to watch videos & play games on internet.

4. Discreet: AutoDesk

Electronic Mail – or e-mail to create messages & send via modem.

1. Outlook Express: Microsoft, handles e-mail & contacts

2. Outlook: Microsoft, a larger version of Outlook Express with contacts, a calendar, task list, journal & notes.

3. Navigator Communicator: Netscape

4. Euduro: Qualcomm. One of 1st e-mail programs available

Web Browsers – Helps connect user to internet & browse it.

1. Internet Explorer: Microsoft

2. Netscape Navigator: Netscape

3. Opera: Opera Software

Utility Tools – programs that help with maintenance of your computer

1. Norton Anti-Virus: Symantec, & is an anti-virus program

2. Norton Utilities: Symantec, for diagnosing & fixing potential computer problems

3. McAfee Anti-Virus: McAfee Enterprises, anti-virus program

Accounting – To calculate financial data

1. Simply Accounting: ACCPAC Corp, for small-medium size businesses.

2. ACCPAC: ACCPAC, for medium-large businesses.

3. QuickBooks: Intuit, small-medium

4. Peachtree: Peachtree Software, small-large

Specialized – programs that target a specific task or market

1. Goldmine: GoldMine Software Corp, contact management program.

2. Money: Microsoft, personal financial management

3. Quicken: Intuit, personal finances

Desktop Properties – to change the settings of your Desktop: Right /a blank area on your Desktop>Properties &…

Theme – changes your windows environment with new colors & Desktop pictures: /Themes *tab*, /Theme *arrow*>Windows Classic…

Custom Desktop – Set background picture & display certain icons: /Desktop *tab*, select a background, /Apply, or /Customize Desktop (b) & check 1 of 4 boxes of the *icons* you want displayed on your Desktop, or set your own Background picture: /Browse (b) & find a picture on your computer, //it, /Apply…

Screen Saver – used to display pretty pictures if computer is inactive after a certain period of time: /Screen Saver *tab*, /Screen saver *arrow*>any & /Preview (b) to see…. Move your mouse to disrupt it. Change the "Wait" time to 10 minutes when computer is inactive it will go to "Screen Saver." Check "On resume…" box so if you're away from your computer for 10 minutes you'll have to log back on (it's good incase you forget to log off & you don't want others to have access to your computer without a password)

Appearance – changes the colors of your windows, font size or smoothness of your text: /Appearance *tab*. If the text below your icons on your Desktop are too small: /Font size *arrow*>a larger size. /Effects (b), /First *arrow*>Scroll Effect (so menus don't fade in like ghosts), /2nd *arrow*>Standard (smoothes your text so it doesn't look to jagged), also if your icons on your Desktop are too small for you: check "Use large icons."

Customize Start Menu – Making it easier to use by pinning in most recent programs used…

Pinning – The Start *menu* has 2 sides: a white & blue, the white is sectioned by faint lines, into 3. The top sections never changes, the middle will typically display the programs you use most recently & hence always rotating, bottom of course is the Green *arrow* for "All Programs." If you know of some programs you'll always be using & you don't want rotated, you can "pin" them permanently to the top section: Find a program anywhere in the white part of the Start *menu*, including its submenu "All Programs," & Right /it>Pin to Start menu.

Taskbar Appearance – Right /Start (b)>Properties /Taskbar *tab* &…

Uncheck "Group similar task buttons" (if you don't like your Taskbar grouping similar programs together in one (b) i.e. say you have 3 documents opened, the Taskbar displays one (b) with the #3 next to it).

Check "Lock the taskbar" (keeps you or other from accidentally expanding the Taskbar or moving it off from the bottom of your screen).

Check "Show Quick Launch" (this is a Toolbar added to the left side of your Taskbar, but if you can / & drag its dotted border all the way right (if your Taskbar isn't locked) – it's a bit tricky if you don't have a steady hand to drag it perfectly horizontal. 3 (b)s are already added to this *toolbar*, but note one is a "Desktop" (b) that when /, it minimizes all your opened programs & / again to maximize them. You can also / & drag other icons to this little *toolbar* to add it as a shortcuts that is activated with a single /. To delete: Right /any shortcut>Delete).

Add Printer – when you buy a new printer, it comes with a CD & a set of instructions & connect to your USB port – which is a plug n play port; follow those, but if that doesn't work & you aren't using USB cable, but a standard 25-pin printer cable, then do the following exercise: /Start (b)>Printers & Faxes, <u>TP</u>: /Add Printer, /Next & select "Local printer…" & uncheck "Automatically detect…" /Next, /Next & select the "Manufacturer" & "Printer" /Next & type in a printer **name**, /Next & if you want others on your next to have access select "Share"

Button (b)	Enter or Return ®	Close X

& type in printer **name**, /Next & type printer's **location**, /Next select "No" for print test page, /Next, /Finish

<u>Connect to Network Printer</u> – to connect to a printer already installed on your network: /Start (b)>Printers & Faxes, /Add Printer, /Next, select "a network printer or a printer attached to another computer," /Next & select "Browse for a printer," /Next & in "Shared printers" *box* //the names to expand (also if expanded it will collapse) more subnames… keep doing it until you see a list of printers, then select one & /Next & follow rest of wizard to install…

<u>Cancel Print Job</u> – to stop printing, either /a Cancel (b) on your printer, or on your Taskbar, next to your computer's clock, //Printer *icon* to open Print Queue (if you don't see on then it may have already printed) & Right /your print job>Cancel, or…

<u>Print Jobs Accumulating in Print Queue (Stop & restart Spooler)</u> – if you see in your Print Queue other people's documents accumulating, but not printing, then: Right /My Computer>Manage, //Services & Applications to expand it, select "Services," & in details *pane* find & Right /Print Spooler>Stop, then Right /it again>Start.

Sharing Files – default folder is already set up to share among others on your network: /Start (b)>My Computer (Note: Shared Documents *folder* is being shared currently as it has a hand underneath the folder). Anything you put into the "Shared Documents" *folder* will be placed on the network for others to access & use. For them to access that *folder* they can: /Start (b)>My Network Places… To remove this folder from being shared, or prevent others from making changes to your files inside the "Shared Folder" then: Right /Shared Documents *folder*> Sharing & Security…

Remote Connection – you can connect to your work computer from home or vice versa & work on it. Note: once you connect to your work computer from home, it will lock your work computer from anybody else using it. 2nd Note: but if someone at your work knows your password & logs on while you're working on it remotely from home, you'll be bumped off.

1. You must make sure that the computer you want to remotely connect to (i.e. you computer at work, so you can work from home) has & you know its "Name," log on "User Name," "Password," and "Domain Name." (Note: the computer name & domain name you can get one of two ways, either ask your IT person, or find out yourself: Right /My Computer>Properties, /Computer Name *tab*, & from the "Computer description" *box* write down the name (Note: there's a "Full computer name" but sometimes that name ends with a 3 # or letter suffix that won't work i.e. kirt computer.kcd), /Change (b) & look in the *section* "Member of" & write down the Domain or Workgroup name to use in the next steps).

   a. Also, the computer at your work (the one you want to remotely connect to), has to be quickly programmed to allow you (from your computer at home) to access it: On your "Work" computer, Right /My Computer>Properties, /Remote *tab* & check "Allow users to connect…" /ok

2. Now, on you home computer you can connect it by: /Start (b)>All Programs>Accessories>Communications>Remote Desktop Connection, /Options (b) (to expand & view list of options), /Experience *tab*, /arrow>your connection speed, /Local

| Mouse Click / | To > | Task Pane <u>TP</u> |

Resources *tab* & check "Disk Drives" if you want access to those on your remote computer, /General *tab* & enter your work's

  a. **Computer's Name**
  b. **User Name**
  c. **Password**
  d. **Domain Name** (or Workgroup name)...

After you have all that info entered, /Connect (b)... (Note: you'll see your computer on your screen & on the top is a bar where you can /X to close your session when you're finished)

Search Internet – To search the internet to find products or information: Open Internet Explorer & up on address bar type in **www.msn.com** ® & in its search *field* type a **product** & /Search. Other websites that have search fields to type in your searches are: www.google.com, www.altavista.com & there's more.

> Add Favorites – To have Internet Explorer remember your favorite web pages: 1st go to that website /Favorites>Add To Favorites & type in a **name** for it, /ok

> Organize Favorites – To create folders for, delete or move your favorite list of websites: Favorites>Organize Favorites. /& drag to move your favorites in the order you'd like including creating a folder to categorize them in, & then you can / & drag them into the *folder* (Note: some folders will already be there in your list such as the 'Links' *folder*; when you put you links into this folder it creates a shortcut to that link on your Internet Explorer's Link *toolbar*)

> Properties – To customize your homepage settings more: With Internet Explorer open, Tools>Internet Options & in Home Page address *field* type in a **website** that every time you open the internet it takes you there automatically.

Instant Messaging – send messages instantly over the internet...

> Hotmail – Before you can use MSN Messenger you have to have a Hotmail or .NET Passport account (When you sign up for Hotmail it also acts as a .NET Passport account): Go to the website **www.msn.com** & /Hot Mail *link*, /New Account Sign Up *link* and follow direction to obtain your Hotmail account.

> Windows Messenger – /Start>All Programs>Online Services (Or Windows Messenger)> Windows Messenger and it ought to automatically pull up Windows Messenger & sign you in (Note: if it doesn't, it may ask you for your hotmail address to get you set up, simply follow it's instructions).

>> Add Contacts – Adding other people to instant message to, in your contacts book: Bottom of your Windows Messenger *window* /+Add a Contact *link*, select "By e-mail address or sign-in name" /Next, type in **email address** /Next, /Finish.

>>> Remove Contact – Tools>Manage Contacts>Delete Contact...

>>> Send An Instant Message – /Send an Instant Message *link*, & select a person you want to instant message, /ok, a new *window* will open up and you can start typing in your message & hit ® or /Send (b) (Note: you can close your smaller slimmer window and it will minimize to bottom-right of your Task Bar, called the System Tray, and when you want to bring it back Right / the green person *icon*>Open). Note: you can minimize your conversation *window* also to the Taskbar and when you get IM (Instant

| Button (b) | Enter or Return ® | Close X |

Message) it will flash red & a little window will pop up.

File Attachments – to attach a file to your instant message: in Conversation *window* /Send a File or Photo *link* & browse to find one & //it to send.

Status – is to let your contacts know if you're busy: If your Windows Messenger is opened, up at top /the *arrow* next to your name>a choice i.e. busy, out to lunch etc. or, you can Right /the green person *icon* below in the System Tray>My Status>busy and your contacts won't be able to send you and IM.

Preferences – to set you IM options: In Windows Messenger *window* Tools> Options, /Preferences *tab*, here you can increase or decrease the minutes to display the Status "Away" if your haven't been using IM lately (Note: if you don't use your IM, you lose contact until you change your status from "Away" to "Online.")

Remote Assistance – used to help another computer, at user's request during an IM where helper can take control of your computer while you watch or interact along to:

You – Open up your Instant Messenger & Right /a contact>Ask for remote assistance

Help – Help person accepts the invitation & a blank screen opens on his computer

You – /Yes to "…let this person view your screen and chat with you."

Help – Can now see your computer & view your problem & Instant Message you solutions, or on his *toolbar* he can /Take Control…

You – /Yes to "…let him share control of your computer."

When you're done you or Help can /Disconnect! (Note: if it doesn't work, then on both computers: /Start (b), Right /My Computer>Properties, /Remote *tab* & make sure "Allow Remote Assistance…" is checked. 2nd Note: computers that are on the same network i.e. within your company or home are more likely to succeed in the connections; where as different networks may fail a few times before connecting, if at all!)

Disk Cleanup – /Start (b)>Control Panel, /Performance & Maintenance, /Free up space on your hard disk, /ok, then select each one & view description below to know what it does… then check appropriate ones & /ok, /Yes

Defragmenter – improves performance & life of your Hard Disk by allowing more efficient storage of files, which means: less physical wear & tear on heads, faster OS & application startup, performance & quick file retrieval. In other words, Windows OS writes data in small pieces on your Hard Disk, & tries to keep them close together for quick retrieval, but as disk fills up & files are added & removed, these files become scattered or fragmented all over the disk, & that requires more work from drive: /Start (b)>Control Panel, /Performance & Maintenance, /Rearrange items on your hard disk…, select drive C:, /Analyze (this will take a minute & will tell you how much of your disk is fragmented), /View Report (to see details of analysis. Note: scroll down in the report & if "Fragmented" = more that 5% then, it's a good idea to defrag) /Defragment (b) (Note: this can take several hours, & if terminated in middle you won't hurt it, but lose ALL & have to redo it over later)

Backup & Restore Files – Insert tape or floppy if you plan to back up on them…

    <u>Backup</u> – /Start>Control Panel, /Performance & Maintenance, /Back up your data, /Next & select Backup, /Next & on "What To Back Up," page select an option, /Next…

        IF – you chose, "Let Me Choose," expand source location of files & check boxes you want backed up, /Next…

        …/Select The Backup Type *arrow*>a type i.e. tape, otherwise your only choice will be file, /Choose A Place To Save Your Backup *arrow*>tape or floppy, enter a **name** for backup, /Next, /Finish OR, /Advanced & select a type of backup to perform i.e. incremental or daily etc., /Next & check any options, /Next & select append or replace, /Next…

        IF – now, /Finish.

        IF – later, then enter a job name, /Set Schedule & select an option…

            IF – daily, weekly or monthly, /Advanced & configure properties, /ok…

            IF – you want to run on more than one schedule (i.e. daily & monthly), check "Show Multiple Schedules," & /New (to create additional schedules)

        …/ok, /Next, in "Run As," *box* type user **name** & password (one who has permissions to backup), /ok, /Finish

    <u>Archive File Attribute</u> – is assigned to every file created in Windows in file's Properties. User can uncheck it after it's backed up so it doesn't keep getting backed up.

        <u>Backup Types</u> – Windows has 4 types

            1. <u>Copy</u> – Backs up all or some files, & doesn't clear Archive attribute from files

            2. <u>Full</u> – Backs up all or some files & clears Archive from all files

            3. <u>Incremental</u> – Backs up all files since last full or incremental & clears all Archive

            4. <u>Differential</u> – Backs up all files since last full backup & doesn't clear Archive

            5. <u>Daily</u> – Backs up files created or modified on day backup is performed & doesn't clear Archive

    <u>Restore</u> – Load your backup media (tape), /Start>Control Panel, /Performance & Maintenance, /Back up your data, /Next & select Restore, /Next & below "Items to Restore," expand backup media (file or tape) & expand backup set you want to restore, & check what you want restored, /Next & /Advanced to set destination, overwriting etc., /Finish

System Restore – you can restore your computer to an earlier time when it was working properly & the good thing is that it won't erase your files, but only remove programs that at one point messed up your system: /Start (b)>Control Panel, /Performance & Maintenance <u>TP</u>: /System Restore, /Next & select a date (Note: only dates in **bold** are actually "Check Points" that you can choose to restore you computer to), /Next, /Next… & computer will take a few minutes & reboot to your restore date.

Create Restore Point – restore points are typically saved when you shut down your computer, but it is recommended that before you add any new program to your computer that you create a "Restore Point," in case the program you installed fowls up your computer. To create: Start>Control Panel, /Performance & Maintenance TP: /System Restore & select "Create a restore point," /Next & type in a **description** of you restore point i.e. **before upgrading to Windows 2006 Longhorn**, /Create…

Shortcuts

Ctrl+// a *folder* within a *folder* – Opens that 2nd *folder* up with its own window

Ctrl+Alt+Delete – When programs freeze up, this shortcut will present a pop up window and tell you what programs are "not responding":

1. First select Program "Not Responding" & /End Task (b) & wait for a minute. If after a couple attempts to End Task doesn't work then…

2. /Start (b)>Turn off Computer, /Turn Off, & wait a minute, & if computer doesn't shut down then…

3. Push and hold Power (b) on computer until it shuts off (about 6-7 seconds)

Alt+Tab – alternate between 2 or more opened programs

Print Scrn – copies screen, & then you can open a word document & /Paste (b)

Alt+Print Scrn – copies only active window, & then you can open a word document & /Paste (b)

Ctrl+Alt+S – pulls up model & Product # of your computer (Note: only works on some)

Ctrl+Z – Undo any action

Ctrl+Y – Redo any undid action.

Ctrl+S – *Save*

Ctrl+X – *Cut*

Ctrl+C – *Copy*

Ctrl+V – *Paste*

Computer Purchasing

	Low-end	Mid-range	High-end
Cost	$600–$800	$800–$1,500	$1,500+
CPU Speed	2.4–2.6 GHz	2.8–3.0 GHz	3.4 GHz+
RAM	256 MB	512 MB	1 GB+
Hard Disk	120 GB	120–160 GB	200 GB+
Removable Storage	CD-ROM recorder	DVD-ROM recorder	DVD-Double Layer recorder
Video Card RAM	32 MB	64–128 MB	256 MB+
Monitor Size	15"	17"	19" or Larger

About the Author

Early on in his career Kirt Kershaw received "The Distinguished Service Award" from the Jordan School District's Superintendent for successfully help graduating 24 out of 25 at-risk high school students. Realizing his creative outreach skills in communications both written and oral, he applied and got accepted in one of the nation's top journalism schools, the University of Utah.

He graduated there with a BS in Mass Communications, and an emphasis in Broadcast Journalism. His certifications include: Microsoft Office Specialist Master Instructor 2000, XP and Microsoft Office Specialist Master 2003, Microsoft Project XP and A+. He is the President of Dream Force LLC a software training company and can be contacted at 801-278-0892, or found on the Web at www.dreamforce.us.